First World War
and Army of Occupation
War Diary
France, Belgium and Germany

40 DIVISION
Divisional Troops
Divisional Signal Company
1 June 1916 - 31 March 1919

WO95/2601/2

The Naval & Military Press Ltd
www.nmarchive.com
Published in association with The National Archives

Published by

The Naval & Military Press Ltd

Unit 10 Ridgewood Industrial Park,

Uckfield, East Sussex,

TN22 5QE England

Tel: +44 (0) 1825 749494

www.naval-military-press.com

www.nmarchive.com

This diary has been reprinted in facsimile from the original. Any imperfections are inevitably reproduced and the quality may fall short of modern type and cartographic standards.

Contents

War Diary	Haplincourt	19/11/1917	20/11/1917
War Diary	Beaumetz Lez Cambrai	21/11/1917	21/11/1917
War Diary	Havrincourt	22/11/1917	25/11/1917
War Diary	Neuville Bourjonval	26/11/1917	26/11/1917
War Diary	Basseux	27/11/1917	30/11/1917
Diagram etc	Appendix I		
Diagram etc	Appendix II		
Miscellaneous	D.A.G. 3rd Echelon		
War Diary	Basseux	01/12/1917	02/12/1917
War Diary	Behagnies	03/12/1917	14/12/1917
War Diary	Gomiecourt	15/12/1917	31/12/1917
Diagram etc			
War Diary	Gomiecourt	01/01/1918	05/01/1918
War Diary	Behagnies Map Ref 57c M.2.A H. 5	06/01/1918	31/01/1918
Miscellaneous	D.A.G. 3rd Echelon	08/03/1918	08/03/1918
War Diary	Behagnies Ref 57 C 1/40,000 H 2 A 15.55	01/02/1918	12/02/1918
War Diary	Gomiecourt Ref 57 C 1/40,000 A 23 D 5.6	13/02/1918	27/02/1918
War Diary	Basseux Ref 51 C 1/40,000 Q 34 V 5.15	28/02/1918	28/02/1918
Heading	40th Divisional Signal Company R.E. March 1918		
Miscellaneous	D.A.G. 3rd Echelon	19/04/1918	19/04/1918
War Diary	Basseux 51 C Q 34 2.5.15	01/03/1918	20/03/1918
War Diary	Hamelincourt 51B 529 D Central	21/03/1918	22/03/1918
War Diary	Bucquoy 57D L10.V1.8	23/03/1918	25/03/1918
War Diary	Monchy-Au-Bois Lens 11	26/03/1918	26/03/1918
War Diary	Habarcq Lens 11	27/03/1918	27/03/1918
War Diary	Lucheux Lens 11	28/03/1918	29/03/1918
War Diary	Chelers Lens 11	30/03/1918	30/03/1918
War Diary	Chelers	31/03/1918	31/03/1918
Heading	40th Divisional Signal Company R.E. April 1918		
Miscellaneous	D.A.G. 3rd Echelon	13/05/1918	13/05/1918
War Diary	Chelers (Lens II) (Somme)	01/04/1918	01/04/1918
War Diary	Merville Sheet 36 A K29 D1.7 1/40,000	02/04/1918	02/04/1918
War Diary	Croix du Bac Sheet 36 1/40000	03/04/1918	09/04/1918
War Diary	Vieux Berquin Sheet 36a E24 A2.2 1/40,000	10/04/1918	10/04/1918
War Diary	La Mot au Bois 36A D30 D1.2 1/40,000	11/04/1918	11/04/1918
War Diary	Au Souverain 36A D11B Central 1/40,000	12/04/1918	12/04/1918
War Diary	Renescure Sheet 27 T.C15.90 1/40,000	13/04/1918	14/04/1918
War Diary	Longuenesse 27 A.S.E. D15 Central 1/20,000	15/04/1918	15/04/1918
War Diary	Wizernes Sheet 36d N E F 2 D8.O 1/20,000	16/04/1918	16/04/1918
War Diary	Wizernes	17/04/1918	29/04/1918
War Diary	St Omer Sheet 27A SE C12 C5.3 1/20000	30/04/1918	30/04/1918
War Diary	St Omer Map Ref Hazebrouck 5A Scale 1/100,000	01/05/1918	13/05/1918
War Diary	St Omer	14/05/1918	31/05/1918
War Diary	St Omer Sheet 36 D F5 Central 1/40000	01/06/1918	03/06/1918
War Diary	Lederzeele Sheet 27 C22 C 3.0 1/40000	04/06/1918	16/06/1918
War Diary	Lederzeele	17/06/1918	22/06/1918
War Diary	Renescure Sheet 27 T20 D 95 1/40,000	23/06/1918	30/06/1918
War Diary	Renescure Map Ref Sheet 27 SW. 1/20000 T21 C.1.6	01/07/1918	21/08/1918
War Diary	Sheet 27 U. 30 C0.7	22/08/1918	31/08/1918
War Diary	Wallon Cappel U 30 C0.7 Sheet 27	01/09/1918	02/09/1918
War Diary	La Motte (D30 C6.4) Sheet 27	03/09/1918	29/09/1918
War Diary	A21A6.7 Sheet 36 NW.	30/09/1918	13/10/1918
War Diary	A21a 6.7	14/10/1918	18/10/1918
War Diary	Armentieres	19/10/1918	20/10/1918
War Diary	Mouveaux	21/10/1918	26/10/1918
War Diary	Lannoy	27/10/1918	18/11/1918

War Diary	Roubaix	19/11/1918	31/01/1919
War Diary	Roubaix Sheet 37 NW	01/02/1919	28/02/1919
Miscellaneous	DAG 3rd Echelon	05/04/1919	05/04/1919
War Diary	Roubaix 36/25 B20.70	01/03/1919	27/03/1919
War Diary	Roubaix	28/03/1919	31/03/1919

40TH DIVISION

40TH DIVL SIGNAL COY R.E.

JUN 1916 - MAR 1919.

Box 2601

ORIGINAL

Confidential

Instructions regarding War Diaries and Intelligence Summaries are contained in F. S. Regs., Part II. and the Staff Manual respectively. Title Pages will be prepared in manuscript.

40th Divl Sig Coy R.E.

WAR DIARY or ~~INTELLIGENCE SUMMARY~~

(Erase heading not required.)

June 1916

Army Form C. 2118

40 Div Sig Co

Vol 1

Place	Date	Hour	Summary of Events and Information	Remarks and references to Appendices
	1.6.16.	4.5pm	Entrained at Farnborough – Hqrs & No1 Section.	
	2.6.16.	12 noon	Disembarked at Le Havre – Hdqrs & No1 Section	
		3 pm	Entrained at Farnborough No 2 Section.	
	3.6.16.	2.19pm	Entrained at Le Havre – Hdqrs & No1 Section	
			Entrained at Farnborough – No 3 Section.	
NORRENT-FONTES	4.6.16.	9.30am	Detrained LILLERS – Hdqrs & No1 Section	
			Entrained at Walsing – No 4 Section	
			Telephone line between YD2 & AAR & LRS provided by 1st Army on AL 9 & 10	
	5.6.16		Telephone line with CRA by cable established late in evening – FONTAINE-LEZ-HERMANS	
	6.6.16		Line ZKI in morning & ZLZ in evening on AL 7 & 8.	
			Line CRE at LIGNY-LES-AIRE at 12 noon	
			Local telephones – G Branch, G.O.C., Q Branch, A.P.M.,	
	7.6.16.		CRA line very noisy, due to power, improved by 1A Section.	
	8.6.16.		2nd Lt R.B. Lister reported for duty, and 2nd Lt Gardiner from 1st Corps.	
	9.6.16.		No2 Section to HOUCHIN, Sappers Fraser & Mackinlay joined them.	
	10.6.16.		No2 Section to BULLY GRENAY.	
	11.6.16.		Lt G.J. Websdale joined from 12th Divl Sig Coy R.E.	
	12.6.16.		Two operators to FONTAINE-LEZ-HERMANS to R.A. office.	
	13.6.16		—	
	14.6.16.		Time advanced one hour.	
	15.6.16.		2nd Lt LISTER went sick.	
	16.6.16 17.6.16 18.6.16		Advanced party to BRUAY under Lt WEBSDALE, office open 7.35 pm.	
BRUAY	19.6.16.		Marched to BRUAY, staff arrived 12 noon.	
" " "	20.6.16 21.6.16 22.6.16		119th Bde office opened at MARLES-LES-MINES, sounder superimposed on telephone pair. ZKI-WEB line to DIVION.	

1875 Wt. W593/826 1,000,000 4/15 J.B.C. & A. A.D.S.S./Forms/C. 2118.

2

ORIGINAL

Confidential

Instructions regarding War Diaries and Intelligence Summaries are contained in F. S. Regs., Part II. and the Staff Manual respectively. Title Pages will be prepared in manuscript.

Army Form C. 2118

40th Divisional Signal Company R.E WAR DIARY or ~~INTELLIGENCE~~ SUMMARY

(Erase heading not required.)

Place	Date	Hour	Summary of Events and Information	Remarks and references to Appendices
BRUAY ~~23.6.16~~	23/6/16		—	
"	24/6/16.		120th Bde office open at BRUAY	
"	25/6/16		121st Bde office open at BULLY-GRENAY in communication with YA.	
"	26/6/16.		—	
"	27/6/16.		Laid cable DIVION to MARLES-LES-MINES.	
"	28/6/16		2nd Corpl Brown to 1st Div, for buried cable instruction. LceCpl Keighley + Pnr Lupton to 1st Corps for lineman's instruction.	
"	29/6/16		1st Corps instructing an airline detachment of No1 Section.	
"	30/6/16		Uneventful.	

40th Divisional Signal Coy. No. Date 1/7/16. R. E.

[signature] Capt R.E

O. COMMANDING 40TH SIGNAL COY. ROYAL ENGINEERS.

1875 Wt. W593/826 1,000,000 4/15 J.B.C. & A. A.D.S.S./Forms/C. 2118.

ORIGINAL SECRET

Instructions regarding War Diaries and Intelligence Summaries are contained in F. S. Regs., Part II. and the Staff Manual respectively. Title Pages will be prepared in manuscript.

WAR DIARY
or
~~INTELLIGENCE SUMMARY~~
(Erase heading not required.)

40TH DIVL. SIGNAL COY., R.E.
JULY 1916

40 July

Army Form C. 2118

Vol. 2

Place	Date July	Hour	Summary of Events and Information	Remarks and references to Appendices
BRUAY	1		Airline party to 1st Corps for instruction. LT Websdale completed test board.	
"	2		Uneventful	
"	3		121st Bde Hdqrs moved to LE BREBIS, took over 2B office.	
			119th Bde Hdqrs moved to BARLIN, took over 2LA office.	
			121st Bde relieved 2nd Bde in trenches.	
			Advanced party under LT WEBSDALE moved to NOEUX LES MINES, & began taking over office at 12 midnight.	
NOEUX-LES-MINES	4		120th Bde Hdqrs moved to LE BREBIS, & took over 2C office.	
			119th Bde do do, & took over 2A office.	
			Remainder of Company, less one relief in office, moved to NOEUX-LES-MINES, office taken over 11 pm.	
"	5		Last office relief arrived from BRUAY.	
			Artillery offices and exchanges, completed taking over at midday.	
"	6.		Fitted two new exchange boards in left Central Artillery Exchange.	
"	7.		} Uneventful	
"	8		}	
"	9		New exchange board in Right O P Exchange fitted.	
"	10		Uneventful	
"	11		Relief of 121st by 120th Bde in MAROC Sector completed 11 pm.	
"	12		1st Corps building new semi-permanent route to Le BREBIS.	
"	13		do do.	
"	14		above completed	
"	15		Uneventful	
"	16		New buried route Right Bde to CALONNE completed.	
"	17		Changed office at night.	

ORIGINAL

SECRET

Instructions regarding War Diaries and Intelligence Summaries are contained in F. S. Regs., Part II. and the Staff Manual respectively. Title Pages will be prepared in manuscript.

WAR DIARY
or
~~INTELLIGENCE SUMMARY~~
(Erase heading not required.)

40TH DIVL. SIGNAL COY. R.E.
JULY 1916

Army Form C. 2118

Page 2

Place	Date	Hour	Summary of Events and Information	Remarks and references to Appendices
NOEUX-LES-MINES	19		Uneventful	
"	20		121st opened report centre in MAROC 9.30 pm, closed next morning 3.45 am.	
"	21		Commenced to take over LOOS Sector.	
"	22		LOOS Sector taken over. 120th Bde relieved 119th in CALONNE sector.	
"	23		Left Artillery subgroup established with central Exchange in N.E MAROC.	
"	24		1st Corps completing new permanent for leading into office from railway.	
"	25		No 1 Buried pair PHILOSOPHE to LOOS taken into use.	
"	26		} Uneventful	
"	27		}	
"	28		Do	
"	29		Do	
"	30		119th Bde relieved 120th Bde in ~~MAR~~ CALONNE Sector. Buried route BULLY-CALONNE completed.	
"	31		Uneventful	

[signature]
Capt. R.E.
O. Commanding
40TH SIGNAL COY. ROYAL ENGINEERS.

40
Div Signals
Vol 3

CONFIDENTIAL

War Diary
of
40th Divisional Signal Company R.E.

from 1st August 1916 to 31st August 1916.

SECRET

DUPLICATE

AUGUST 1916 WAR DIARY or INTELLIGENCE SUMMARY

40TH DIVL. SIGNAL COY. R.E.

Army Form C. 2118

Instructions regarding War Diaries and Intelligence Summaries are contained in F. S. Regs., Part II. and the Staff Manual respectively. Title Pages will be prepared in manuscript.

(Erase heading not required.)

Place	Date	Hour	Summary of Events and Information	Remarks and references to Appendices
NOEUX-LES-MINES	1		Uneventful.	
"	2		Cable routes in CALONNE Sector for telephone post scheme fixed. LOOS Test point to Left Battn route proceeding.	
"	3		Section for telephone post scheme to CALONNE	
"	4		LT HORNBLOWER working on Telephone Post Scheme Calonne. Lt RICE-JONES joining up night group RA on new buried lines.	
"	5		Do	
"	6		Infantry working party commenced work on telephone post scheme CALONNE.	
"	7		Connecting up buried route to O Pexchange + O Ps in CALONNE.	
"	8		Uneventful	
"	9		LOOS Sub-sector handed over to left-flank division. Spare cable in CALONNE N cleaned up.	
	10		Uneventful	
"	11		Capt WEBBSDALE reviewing the LE BREBIS divisional office.	
"	12		121st Bde relieved 120th Bde in the MAROC Subsector	
"	13		Uneventful	
"	14		Do	
"	15		LE BREBIS shelled, several airlines + E buried route broken.	
"	16		} Uneventful	
"	17			
"	18		Laid airlines for Watersupply company. Lines of CALONNE Telephone Post Scheme completed.	
"	19		Commenced digging for MAROC Telephone Posts under 2nd Lt APPLEYARD.	
"	20		Digging in MAROC	
"	21			
"	22		Reml O.Ps connected up. TP lines in CALONNE taken into use.	

1875 Wt. W593/826 1,000,000 4/15 J.B.C. & A. A.D.S.S./Forms/C. 2118.

SECRET

Instructions regarding War Diaries and Intelligence Summaries are contained in F. S. Regs., Part II. and the Staff Manual respectively. Title Pages will be prepared in manuscript.

DUPLICATE

AUGUST 1916

WAR DIARY
or
~~INTELLIGENCE SUMMARY~~

(Erase heading not required.)

40TH DIVL SIGNAL COY R.E.

Army Form C. 2118

Place	Date	Hour	Summary of Events and Information	Remarks and references to Appendices
NOEUX-LES-MINES	23		Uneventful	
"	24		Arranging to take over LOOS & 14 BIS Sectors in addition to present front.	
"	25		119th Bde took over LOOS Subsector. LOOS artillery group taken over.	
"	26		112th Bde took over 14 BIS Subsector. 14 BIS " " " ". Took Signals 63rd Divn round CALONNE Subsector.	
"	27		FOSSE 7 to MAROC buried cable line progressing.	
"	28		1st Corps built two pairs LEBREBIS to MAZINGARBE.	
"	29		Handed over diagrams to 63rd Divn of CALONNE Sector.	
"	30		30th Relief of CALONNE Subsector completed. Digging on FOSSE 7 – MAROC dig, 50 Gunners. McKenzie took over MAROC Telephone Pant works.	
"	31		Many lines in MAZINGARBE broken by shell fire and one in NOEUX-LES-MINES.	

[illegible] Capt RE

O. COMMANDING 40TH SIGNAL COY. ROYAL ENGINEERS.

40th Divisional Signal Coy. No. Date 1/9/16 R. E.

1875 Wt. W593/826 1,000,000 4/15 J.B.C. & A. A.D.S.S./Forms/C. 2118.

Officer i/c A.G.'s Office at the Base

~~Officer i/c R.E. Records Chatham~~

Wandering in Original ~~Duplicate~~

forwarded herewith

40th Divisional Signal Coy.
No.
Date 1/10/16
R. E.

[illegible] Capt R.E.
O. COMMANDING
40TH SIGNAL COY. ROYAL ENGINEERS

SECRET

Instructions regarding War Diaries and Intelligence Summaries are contained in F. S. Regs., Part II. and the Staff Manual respectively. Title Pages will be prepared in manuscript.

SEPTEMBER 1916 WAR DIARY ~~or INTELLIGENCE SUMMARY~~

(Erase heading not required.)

40TH DIVL. SIGNAL COY R.E.

ORIGINAL

Army Form C. 2118

40

Vol 4

Place	Date	Hour	Summary of Events and Information	Remarks and references to Appendices
NOEUX-LES-MINES	1st		14 BIS Sub-Sector handed over to 3rd Divn.	
"	2nd		100 men on MAROC Telephone Post Scheme. 75 men on FOSSE 7 – MAROC dig.	
"	3rd		do	
"	4th		do	
"	5th		121st Bde relieved by 120th Bde in MAROC Subsector.	
"	6th		Uneventful	
"	7th–10th		Uneventful	
"	11th		121st Bde relieved 119th Bde in LOOS Subsector	
"	12th–17th		50 Gunners + 100 Infantry working on MAROC telephone posts and FOSSE 7 to ARTILLERY ROW dig.	
"	18th		119th Bde relieved 120th Bde in MAROC.	
"	19th–21st		Uneventful	

1375 Wt. W593/826 1,000,000 4/15 J.B.C. & A. A.D.S.S./Forms/C. 2118.

ORIGINAL

Army Form C. 2118

SECRET

Instructions regarding War Diaries and Intelligence Summaries are contained in F. S. Regs., Part II. and the Staff Manual respectively. Title Pages will be prepared in manuscript.

SEPTEMBER 1916

WAR DIARY
~~or~~
~~INTELLIGENCE SUMMARY~~

(Erase heading not required.)

40TH DIVL. SIGNAL COY R.E.

Place	Date	Hour	Summary of Events and Information	Remarks and references to Appendices
NOEUX-LES-MINES	22nd		Telephone Posts LOOS completed. 120th Bde took over 14 BIS Sector from 3rd Divn.	
"	23rd		Uneventful (23rd–26th)	
"	24th			
"	25th			
"	26th			
"	27th		60 cyclists came from Corps to assist in burying cable. No 1 Section clearing cable out of trenches in 14 BIS Subsector.	
"	28th		Uneventful (28th–30th)	
"	29th			
"	30th			

[illegible] Capt R.E.

O. Commanding 40th Signal Coy. Royal Engineers

1875 Wt. W593/826 1,000,000 4/15 J.B.C. & A. A.D.S.S./Forms/C. 2118.

SECRET

DAG 3rd Echelon Base

~~Col. i/c R.E. Records~~

Herewith War Diary for October in original ~~duplicate~~

40th Divisional Signal Coy. Date 1/11/16 R.E.

W Wedner.
Capt R.E.

O.C. COMMANDING
40TH SIGNAL COY. ROYAL ENGINEERS.

SECRET

Instructions regarding War Diaries and Intelligence Summaries are contained in F. S. Regs., Part II. and the Staff Manual respectively. Title Pages will be prepared in manuscript.

ORIGINAL

OCTOBER 1916 WAR DIARY or ~~INTELLIGENCE~~ SUMMARY

(Erase heading not required.)

40TH DIVL SIGNAL COY R.E.

Army Form C. 2118

Place	Date	Hour	Summary of Events and Information	Remarks and references to Appendices
NOEUX-LES-MINES	1st		Uneventful	
	2nd 3rd 4th 5th 6th 7th 8th		Uneventful	
	9th		FOSSE 7 to MAROC buried route completed.	
	10th		Handed over Right Battalion MAROC to 37th Div. Realigned 6 wire semi-permanent from BREBIS to MAZINGARBE.	
	11th		Opened MAZINGARBE Exchange, closed BREBIS Exchange.	
	12th		119th Bde took over the Right Battalion LOOS. 121st Bde took over 14 BIS Sector. 120th Bde took over HALLUCH Sector.	
	13th 14th 15th 16th 17th		Uneventful	
	18th to 24th		Uneventful	

1875 Wt. W593/826 1,000,000 4/15 J.B.C. & A. A.D.S.S./Forms/C. 2118.

SECRET

ORIGINAL

Instructions regarding War Diaries and Intelligence Summaries are contained in F. S. Regs., Part II. and the Staff Manual respectively. Title Pages will be prepared in manuscript.

OCTOBER 1916

WAR DIARY ~~or INTELLIGENCE SUMMARY~~

(Erase heading not required.)

40TH DIVL SIGNAL COY R.E.

Army Form C. 2118

VOL 5

Place	Date	Hour	Summary of Events and Information	Remarks and references to Appendices
~~25th~~ NOEUX-LES-MINES	25th		72nd Bde relieved 120th in HALLUCH Subsector.	
			120th Bde moved into rest Billets LES BREBIS + PETIT SAINS.	
"	26th		17th Bde arrived MAZINGARBE.	
"	27th		120th Bde marched to BRUAY Area. 17th Bde relieved 121st Bde in 14 BIS Subsector.	
			121st Bde moved in to billets in LES BREBIS and PETIT SAINS.	
"	28th		73rd Bde arrived MAZINGARBE	
"	29th		121st Bde moved to BRUAY Area. 73rd Bde relieved 119th Bde in LOOS Subsector.	
			119th Bde moved into billets LE BREBIS + PETIT SAINS.	
			A few men of 24th Divn arrived and began to take over,	
			Advance party sent to ROLLECOURT	
ROLLECOURT	30th		Office closed at BRAQUEMONT + opened at ROLLECOURT at 10am.	
			24th Divn took over at BRAQUEMONT	
			Company marched off at 8.30 am, arrived GRANDCAMP at 3 pm. Billeted at	
			GRANDCAMP. 119th Bde moved to BRUAY. 121st Bde to CHELERS area.	
"	31st		Halted at GRANDCAMP near ROLLECOURT.	

31/10/16

[signature] Capt R.E.
O.C. 40th Divl Sig Coy R.E.

SECRET

Instructions regarding War Diaries and Intelligence Summaries are contained in F. S. Regs., Part II. and the Staff Manual respectively. Title Pages will be prepared in manuscript.

WAR DIARY

NOVEMBER 1916 ~~or~~

~~INTELLIGENCE SUMMARY~~

(Erase heading not required.)

40TH DIVL SIGNAL COY R.E.

Vol X6

Army Form C. 2118

Place	Date	Hour	Summary of Events and Information	Remarks and references to Appendices
ROLLECOURT	1		119th Bde marched to LA THIEULOYE area. Remainder of Divn halting. Communication provided – Telephone pair with superimposed sounder to AAR. DRLS to Bdes.	
"	2		119th Bde moved to MAISNIL-ST-POL area, 120th Bde to REBREUVE area, 121st Bde to the HOUVIN-HOUVIGNEUL area.	
"	3		Divn halted.	
FROHEN-LE-GRAND	4	10am	Divl Office closed at ROLLECOURT & opened at FROHEN-LE-GRAND.	
BERNAVILLE	5	9.30am	" " " FROHEN-LE-GRAND " " BERNAVILLE.	
"	6		Divn halted. 119th Bde at ATHEUX. 120th Bde RIBEAUCOURT. 121st Bde FIENVILLERS.	
"	7		do	
"	8		Uneventful	
"	9			
"	10			
"	11		120th Bde moved to FIEFFES, advanced party 120th Bde to SAILLY-AU-BOIS.	
"	12		120th Bde to DOULLENS.	
"	13		120th Bde to BAYENCOURT.	
"	14		Two battns 120th Bde took over portion line in front of HEBUTERNE from 148th Bde	
"	15		Relief of 148th Bde by 120th Bde completed, 120th Bde coming under 31st Divn. 119th Bde to WAVANS, 121st Bde to REMAISNIL, Divl HQ to FROHEN-LE-GRAND.	
FROHEN-LE-GRAND	16		Divn halted.	
"	17			
"	18		121st Bde to BOUQDEMAISON, 119th Bde to REMAISNIL.	[signature] Capt. Commdg. 40th Signal Coy. Royal Engineers

1875 Wt. W593/826 1,000,000 4/15 J.B.C. & A. A.D.S.S./Forms/C. 2118.

SECRET

Army Form C. 2118

WAR DIARY ~~or INTELLIGENCE~~ SUMMARY

(Erase heading not required.)

NOVEMBER 1916

40th DIVL SIGNAL COMPANY R.E.

Instructions regarding War Diaries and Intelligence Summaries are contained in F. S. Regs., Part II. and the Staff Manual respectively. Title Pages will be prepared in manuscript.

Place	Date	Hour	Summary of Events and Information	Remarks and references to Appendices
~~FROHEN-LE-GRAND~~	19		121st Bde to SUS ST LEGER, 119th Bde to LESUICH; Divl Hdqrs BOUQUEMAISON 11am.	
BOUQUE-MAISON	20		120th Bde to ST LEGER LES AUTHIE.	
BOUQUEMAISON	21		Halted.	
DOULLENS	22		119th Bde to GEZAINCOURT, 120th Bde to AMPLIER, 121st Bde to AUTHIEULE.	
CANAPLES	23		Whole Division moved	
AILLY-LE-HAUT-CLOCHER	24		Do	
"	25		Halted	
"	26		121st Bde to VAUCHELLES, from PONT REMY	
"	27		Signal Class of two men per battalion opened at Divisional Headquarters	
"	28		Uneventful	
"	29		Cables in AILLY (Div HQ) replaced by G.I airlines	
"	30		Uneventful	

[signature] Capt RE
O. COMMANDING 40TH SIGNAL COY. ROYAL E...

1875 Wt. W593/826 1,000,000 4/15 J.B.C. & A. A.D.S.S./Forms/C. 2118.

~~Officer i/c A.G.'s Office at the Base~~
~~Col i/c R.E. Records~~

War Diary for December 1916,
forwarded herewith.

6/1/17

[illegible] Col R.E.
O.C. 40th Divl Sig Coy R.E.

Instructions regarding War Diaries and Intelligence Summaries are contained in F. S. Regs., Part II. and the Staff Manual respectively. Title Pages will be prepared in manuscript.

SECRET

ORIGINAL

WAR DIARY ~~or~~ INTELLIGENCE ~~SUMMARY~~

(Erase heading not required.)

DECEMBER 1916

40TH DIV. SIGNAL CO. R.E.

Army Form C. 2118

40

Vol 7

Place	Date	Hour	Summary of Events and Information	Remarks and references to Appendices
AILLY	1		Uneventful (1–4)	
-do-	2			
-do-	3			
-do-	4			
-do-	5		Uneventful (5–6)	
-do-	6			
-do-	7		Divisional School established at ALLERY Circuit laid from School to HALLENCOURT.	
-do-	8		Uneventful	
do	9		Company marched ST SAUVEUR	
do	10		Company arrived CHIPILLY under 2nd Lt Appleyard. YDZR opened CHIPILLY at noon 119th Bde opened at ~~camp~~ SAILLY-LAURETTE.	
do	11		121st Bde opened at SAILLY-LAURETTE	
do	12		Uneventful (12–13)	
do	13			
CHIPILLY	14		YDZ opened CHIPILLY 10 am, AILLY office remaining open.	
CHIPILLY	15		AILLY office closed 9 am. 120th Bde opened in camp $1\frac{1}{2}$ miles N.W. of BRAY.	
CHIPILLY	16 to 21		Uneventful. 1 Officer & 6 OR with 178 & 181 Bdes R.F.A. in the line.	

1875 Wt. W593/826 1,000,000 4/15 J.B.C. & A. A.D.S.S./Forms/C. 2118.

SECRET

WAR DIARY

or

~~INTELLIGENCE SUMMARY~~

(Erase heading not required.)

DECEMBER 1916

Army Form C. 2118

Instructions regarding War Diaries and Intelligence Summaries are contained in F. S. Regs., Part II. and the Staff Manual respectively. Title Pages will be prepared in manuscript.

ORIGINAL

40TH DIVL SIGNAL COY RE

Place	Date	Hour	Summary of Events and Information	Remarks and references to Appendices
CHIPILLY	22		Adv Party of 120th Bde to 100 Bde to reconnoitre Right Bde Sector in line.	
"	23		Uneventful	
"	24		Adv Party of 119th Bde to 98 Bde to reconnoitre Left Bde Sector in line, 120 Bde party returned.	
"	25		Uneventful	
"	26		120th Bde office closed at ~~[illegible]~~ BRAY 9.45 am. Opened at Right Bde Hdqrs near LE FOREST.	
			119th Bde Hdqrs opened at BRAY.	
"	27		119th Bde Hdqrs opened in chalkpit, near LE FOREST, - Left Brigade.	
			Advanced party taking over Divl Hdqrs - P.C. BONNET - from 33rd Divn.	
			121st Bde to Camps 17 & 21, Hdqrs BRAY.	
B 21 C S of MAUREPAS	28		Divl Hdqrs opened 8 am at B21C & closed at CHIPILLY. 4th Divn on left & 17th French Divn on Right.	
"	29		Uneventful	
"	30		Do	
"	31		121st Bde relieved in Left Sub-Sector by 119th Bde, Hdqrs LE FOREST	

[illegible] Capt R.E.

O.C. 40th Divl Signal Coy RE

SECRET. Copy No......

40th. Division Machine Gun Battalion Order No 1.

Reference,
Map LENS 11.
1. 100,000.
Map B. Nol. M.G. (attached)

1. (a) The 120th. Machine Gun Company will relieve the 119th. Machine Gun Company in the 3rd. Division Area on 27th. February 1918.
(b) The 121st. Machine Gun Company will relieve the 244th. Machine Gun Company in the 59th. Division area on 27th. February 1918.

2. Details of both reliefs will be arranged between Company Commanders concerned. Reliefs will be completed by 3 p.m.
The completion of relief will be notified by 120th. Machine Gun Company to O/C 3rd. Division Machine Gun Battalion and O/C 40th. Division Machine Gun Battalion by the code word " Cheero "
Completion of relief will be notified by 121st Machine Gun Company to O/C 59th. Division Machine Gun Battalion and O/C 40th. Division Machine Gun Battalion by the code word " Monkey "

3. On relief the 119th. Machine Gun Company will move to their billets - ENNISKILLEN CAMP, ERVILLIERS and 244th. Machine Gun Company will move to DURHAM CAMP B. BOISLEUX.

4. The 120th and 121st. Machine Gun Companies will come under orders of the 3rd. and 59th. Divisions respectively from the moment of marching off from their present billets.
The 119th. and 244th Machine Gun Companies will come under orders of this Division on arrival in their rest billets.

5. Reconnaissance of positions will be made by the Officers of 120th and 121st. Machine Gun Companies on 26th. instant.

6. When in Corps Reserve the 119th Machine Gun Company will be prepared to move at short notice to Battery Positions D. E. F. and G. shewn on attached Map M.G.1. Similarly the 244th. Machine Gun Company will be prepared to mann Battery Positions H.I.J. & K.
Officers of the 119th. and 244th. Machine Gun Companies will make a reconnaissance of Battery Positions D - K on 28th. Instant.

7. Acknowledge.

Major.
25th. Feb. 1918. Cmdg. 40th. Division Machine Gun Battalion.

issued at..........

Copy 1 to G.
2 Q.
3 119th. Bde.
4 120th. Bde.
5 121st. Bde.
6 119th. M.G.Coy.
7 120th. M.G.Coy.
8 121st. M.G.Coy.
9 244th. M.G.Coy.
10 C.R.A.
11 C.R.E.

Copy 12. to Signals.
13 A.D.R.S.
14 D.A.D.V.S.
15 D.A.D.O.S.
16 Train.
17 Supply Column.
18 O/C 3Rd. Div. M.G.Battalion.
19 O/C 59th.Div. M.G.Battalion.
20 &21 War Diary.
22 File.

DAG 3rd Echelon
~~To R.E. Records~~

Herewith War Diary for January 1917

[signature]
Capt R.E.

1/2/17

O.C. 40th Divl Signal Coy R.E.

Instructions regarding War Diaries and Intelligence Summaries are contained in F. S. Regs., Part II. and the Staff Manual respectively. Title Pages will be prepared in manuscript.

SECRET

ORIGINAL

WAR DIARY
or
~~INTELLIGENCE SUMMARY~~
(Erase heading not required.)

JANUARY 1917
40TH DIVL.
SIGNAL COY. R.E.

Army Form C.-2118

Vol 8

Place	Date	Hour	Summary of Events and Information	Remarks and references to Appendices
B21C S of MAUREPAS	1		Uneventful.	
"	2			
"	3			
"	4		120th Bde relieved 179th Bde in Left Sub Sector – Hdqrs ~~CRANIÈRES~~ LE FOREST.	
"	5		Uneventful.	
"	6			
"	7		Uneventful	
"	8		119th Bde relieved 121st Bde in Right Sub-sector – Hdqrs CRANIÈRES	
"	9		Uneventful	
"	10			
"	11			
"	12		121st Bde relieved 120th Bde in Left Subsector – RANCOURT	
"	13		Uneventful	
"	14			
"	15			
"	16			
"	17			
"	18		120th Bde relieved 119th Bde in Right Subsector – BOUCHAVESNES NORTH.	
"	19		Uneventful	

1875 Wt. W593/826 1,000,000 4/15 J.B.C. & A. A.D.S.S./Forms/C. 2118.

Instructions regarding War Diaries and Intelligence Summaries are contained in F. S. Regs., Part II. and the Staff Manual respectively. Title Pages will be prepared in manuscript.

SECRET

ORIGINAL

WAR DIARY
or
~~INTELLIGENCE SUMMARY~~
(Erase heading not required.)

40th Divl SIGNAL COY R.E.

Army Form C. 2118

Place	Date	Hour	Summary of Events and Information	Remarks and references to Appendices
P.C. BONNET B21c S of MAUREPAS	20		} Uneventful	
	21		}	
"	22		119th Bde relieved 121st Bde in RANCOURT SECTOR.	
"	23		} Uneventful	
"	24		}	
"	25		121st Bde moved BRAY (camps 17 & 21) to SAILLY LAURETTE	
"	26		24th Bde moved into camps 17 + 21 21st Bde relieved 120th Bde in BOUCHAVESNES N. Subsector. 25th Bde moved into camps 17 + 21. 120th Bde to SAILLY LAURETTE.	
"	27		25th Bde relieved 119th Bde in RANCOURT Subsector 120th Bde to CORBIE. 119th Bde to SAILLY LAURETTE. 8th Divn Advanced Party, taking over offices + lines.	
"	28	10.30am	Handed over at P.C. BONNET to 8th Divn. Opened at CORBIE.	
	29		} Uneventful	
	30		}	
	31		}	

[illegible]
Capt R.E.
O.C. 40th Divl Sig Coy R.E.

1875 Wt. W593/826 1,000,000 4/15 J.B.C. & A. A.D.S.S./Forms/C. 2118.

A.G.'s Office at the Base

~~O i/c R.E. Record~~

War Diary for February 1917 herewith

3.3.17

W. Widnes. Capt R.E.
O.C. 40th Divl Signal Coy R.E.

Instructions regarding War Diaries and Intelligence Summaries are contained in F. S. Regs., Part II. and the Staff Manual respectively. Title Pages will be prepared in manuscript.

SECRET

FEBRUARY 1917

ORIGINAL

WAR DIARY or INTELLIGENCE SUMMARY

(Erase heading not required.)

40TH DIVL SIGNAL COY R.E.

Army Form C. 2118

40

Vol 9

Place	Date	Hour	Summary of Events and Information	Remarks and references to Appendices
CORBIE	1 to 9		Uneventful, in rest.	
"	10		119th Bde from SAILLY LAURETTE to Camps 17 & 21, hdqrs BRAY.	
"	11		119th Bde take over RANCOURT Subsector	
			120th Bde to Camp 111, Hdqrs Camp 111.	
			121st Bde to Camp 21, hdqrs BRAY.	
P.C. BONNET	12		YDZ opened at BRAY, YDZR at P.C. BONNET 10 am.	
"	13 to 19		Uneventful	
"	20		8th Div relieved 4th Div on our right; Guards still on left.	
"	21		121st Bde commenced relief of 119th Bde in RANCOURT Sector.	
"	22		Relief of 119th Bde by 121st completed. 119th Bde Hdqrs BRAY	
"	23 to 28th		Uneventful	

W. Widmer Capt R.E.
O.C. 40th Div Signal Coy
R.E.

1875 Wt. W593/826 1,000,000 4/15 J.B.C. & A. A.D.S.S./Forms/C. 2118.

SECRET

Instructions regarding War Diaries and Intelligence Summaries are contained in F. S. Regs., Part II. and the Staff Manual respectively. Title Pages will be prepared in manuscript.

MARCH 1917

WAR DIARY
~~or~~
~~INTELLIGENCE SUMMARY~~

(Erase heading not required.)

40TH DIVL SIGNAL COY R.E.

Army Form C. 2118

Vol 10

Place	Date	Hour	Summary of Events and Information	Remarks and references to Appendices
P.C. BONNET (S of MAUREPAS)	1		121st Bde holding RANCOURT Sector; 120th bde Div. Reserve, hdqrs BRAY; 119th Bde Hdqrs Camp 112 (N of BRAY).	
"	2 to 5		Uneventful as regards this divn, on morning of 3rd 8th Divn took PALLAS & FRITZ trenches, heavy fighting all day on col just E of BOUCHAVESNES.	
	6		Advance parties of HQ Section, 119th Bde Section and 120th Bde Section reconnoitred lines in CURLU - CLERY area.	
	7		Commenced to take over from 8th Division at P.C. CHAPEAU, CURLU.	
P.C. CHAPEAU (CURLU)	8		Opened office at P.C. CHAPEAU at 8.a.m. Offices at BRAY and MAUREPAS closed at 10.a.m.	
"	9		Transferred 33rd Divisional Signal system complete from P.C. JEAN to P.C. CHAPEAU. Completed by 10.a.m. Opened advanced exchange at FEUILLERES.	
"	10		Improved local lines & picked up a large quantity of old cable.	
"	11 to 14		Do	
"	15		121st Bde relieved 119th Bde in CLERY Sector.	
"	16		Enemy retiring on whole front.	
"	17		Patrols entered MONT ST QUENTIN, HALLE, PERONNE, ALLAINES, up to Hill 115.	
"	18		Signal office opened with outpost company MONT ST QUENTIN. Corps cavalry patrols to BUSSU. 120th Bde moved report centre to P.C. VIOLET, N of CLERY.	

SECRET

Instructions regarding War Diaries and Intelligence Summaries are contained in F. S. Regs., Part II. and the Staff Manual respectively. Title Pages will be prepared in manuscript.

WAR DIARY
~~or~~
ORIGINAL ~~INTELLIGENCE SUMMARY~~

MARCH 1917

(Erase heading not required.)

40TH DIVL SIGNAL COY RE.

Army Form C. 2118

40th Divisional Signal Coy. R.E.

Place	Date	Hour	Summary of Events and Information	Remarks and references to Appendices
P.C. CHAPEAU (NURLU)	19		Corps Cavalry went forward at daybreak to reconnoitre up to DRIENCOURT – LIERAMONT line. Visual terminal watching high ground to East from high ground W of ALLAINES. One Motor Cyclist attached to cavalry to bring reports to Signal station at MONT ST QUENTIN.	
			Outpost line established along NURLU – MONT ST QUENTIN Ridge, to hill 75. Line by flag lamp & telephone.	
P.C. CHAPEAU	20		119th Bde less 2 Bns relieving 120th Bde less 2 Bns in left Sector. NURLU clear of enemy in morning.	
"	21		119th Bde Hdqrs moved to HAUT ALLAINES.	
"	22		181st Bde R.F.A. hdqrs to HAUT ALLAINES, 178th Bde RFA Hdqrs to Mt St Quentin. Communication by permanent line to CLERY, cable to HAUT ALLAINES, & FEUILLAUCOURT. Comic air line – two pairs – FEUILLAUCOURT to MONT ST QUENTIN. Cable to battalions, visual to outpost companies.	
"	23			
"	24		Permanent line completed to FEUILLAUCOURT. 40th Divn front taken over by 3rd Corps, 48th Divn. 119th Bde Hdqrs to LE FOREST. 121st Bde Hdqrs	
"	25		remaining at P.C. WORZEL, CLERY. 120th Bde at OUVRAGES (HEM Wood)	
"	26		Recovering cable.	

1875 Wt. W593/826 1,000,000 4/15 J.B.C. & A. A.D.S.S./Forms/C. 2118.

SECRET

Instructions regarding War Diaries and Intelligence Summaries are contained in F. S. Regs., Part II. and the Staff Manual respectively. Title Pages will be prepared in manuscript.

ORIGINAL

WAR DIARY ~~or INTELLIGENCE SUMMARY~~

MARCH 1917

(Erase heading not required.)

40TH DIVL SIGNAL COY R.E.

Army Form C. 2118.

Place	Date	Hour	Summary of Events and Information	Remarks and references to Appendices
P.C. JEAN (Ecl(URLU)	27		Vacated P.C. CHAPEAU for 15th Corps Hdqrs. Moved Divl Hdqrs to P.C. JEAN	
"	28.		Uneventful	
"	29.		XVth Corps Hdqrs to P.C. CHAPEAU.	
"	30		} Uneventful	
"	31		}	

W Widdows. Capt R.E.
O.C. 40th Divl Signal Coy R.E.

40th Divisional Signal Coy.
No. ....
Date ....
R. E.

2449 Wt. W14957/M90 750,000 1/16 J.B.C. & A. Forms/C.2118/12.

SECRET

Instructions regarding War Diaries and Intelligence Summaries are contained in F. S. Regs., Part II. and the Staff Manual respectively. Title Pages will be prepared in manuscript.

APRIL 1917 **WAR DIARY** ~~or INTELLIGENCE SUMMARY~~ (Erase heading not required.)

Original

40TH DIVL SIGNAL COY R.E.

Vol XI

Army Form C. 2118

Place	Date	Hour	Summary of Events and Information	Remarks and references to Appendices
P.C. JEAN (near CURLU)	1		Lt Summers & Cable Sections marched to MANANCOURT.	
			Hq 119th Bde LE FOREST, 120th Bde OUVRAGES, 121st Bde OMMIECOURT.	
"	2		Building 3 pairs MANANCOURT – EQUANCOURT – FINS.	
"	3		} Uneventful	
"	4			
"	5		One office relief to MANANCOURT, to fit up new office.	
MANANCOURT	6		YDZ closed P.C. JEAN opened at MANANCOURT 4 pm. 121st Bde at FINS.	
			178 + 181 Bdes R.F.A at FINS.	
"	7		119th Bde to ETRICOURT, 120th Bde remaining at P.C. OUVRAGES.	
			8th Divn on Right & 20th Divn on left at ROCQUIGNY.	
			Laying new lines & straightening up, flank lines etc.	
"	8			
"	9		8th Divn moved to GURLU WOOD.	
"	10		Poling lines and straightening up.	
"	11		Do. Snow in evening.	
"	12		} Uneventful	
"	13			
"	14			
"	15		120th Bde moved to EQUANCOURT	
"	16		119th Bde went in line on right of 121st Bde taking over part of 8th Divn front, headquarters ETRICOURT.	
"	17			
"	18-20		Uneventful. 120th Bde relieved 121st Bde on left.	

SECRET

Instructions regarding War Diaries and Intelligence Summaries are contained in F. S. Regs., Part II. and the Staff Manual respectively. Title Pages will be prepared in manuscript.

APRIL 1917

WAR DIARY
or
~~INTELLIGENCE SUMMARY~~
(Erase heading not required.)

40TH DIVL SIGNAL COY R.E.

Army Form C. 2118.

Place	Date	Hour	Summary of Events and Information	Remarks and references to Appendices
MANANCOURT	21	4.20am	119th Bde attacked 15 RAVINE and occupied line running in front of VILLERS PLOUICH & BEAUCAMP.	
			8th Divn took GONNELIEU on our right.	
"	24	4.15am	119th & 120th Bde attacked VILLERS PLOUICH & BEAUCAMP & took up line in front of them.	
"	25		20th Divn took BILHEM & 120th Bde consolidated in front of BEAUCAMP.	
			Two front line battalion of 120th Bde relieved by two of 121st Bde	
"	26		Relief of 120th Bde by 121st completed.	
"	30		Relief of 121st Bde by 120th Bde commenced.	
			For operations 24th & onwards all forward communication from Divl Hdqrs to Brigade Report Centres was airline — one 8 wire route on loop poles + 105 insulators, one two wire route on airline poles ebonite insulators, and an 8 wire lateral route on loop poles & 105 insulators, with 60 lb G.I. wire.	
			5.5.17	
			[illegible] Major RE. O.C. 40th Divl Signal Coy R.E.	

2449 Wt. W14957/M90 750,000 1/16 J.B.C. & A. Forms/C.2118/12.

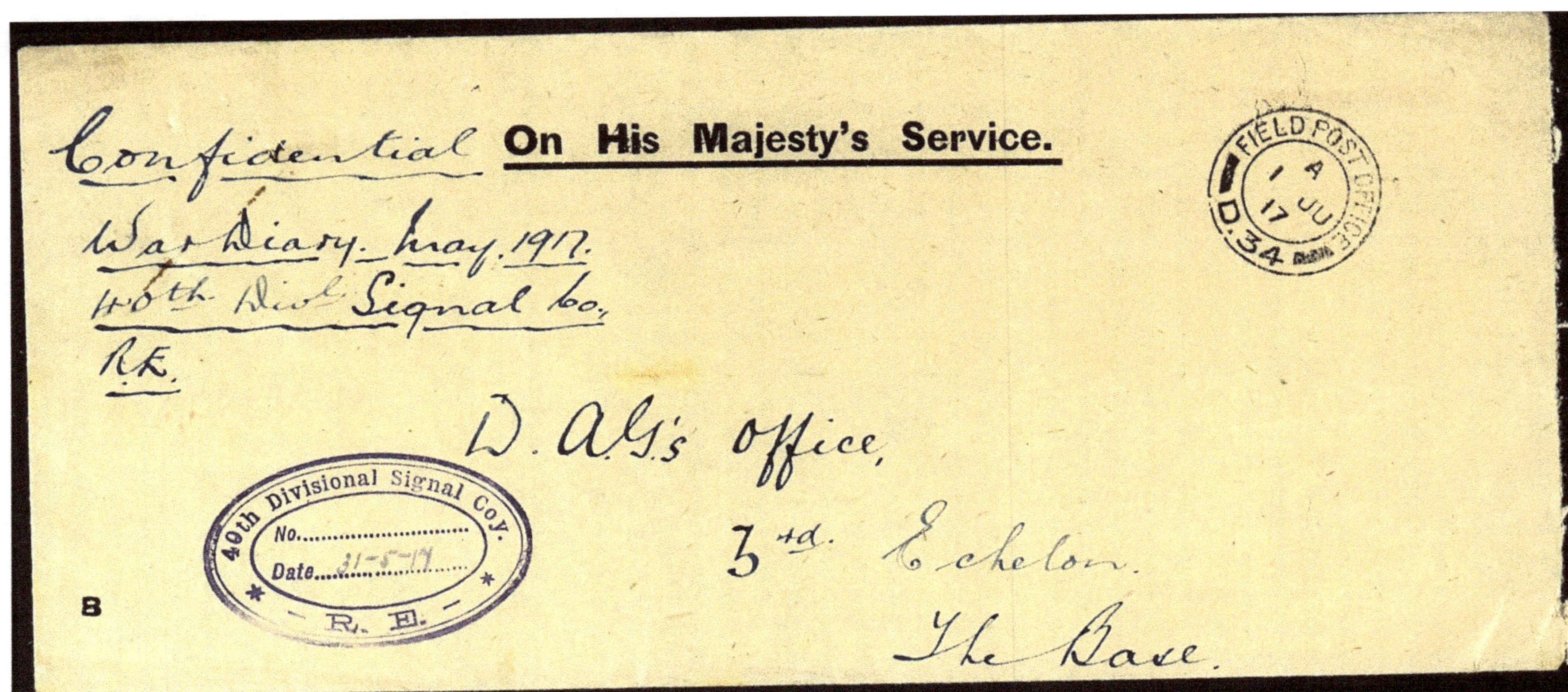
Confidential On His Majesty's Service.

War Diary. May. 1917.
40th Divl. Signal Co.,
R.E.

FIELD POST OFFICE
1 A
1 JU 17
D.34

D.A.G.'s Office,
3rd Echelon.
The Base.

40th Divisional Signal Coy.
No.
Date 31-5-17
R.E.

B

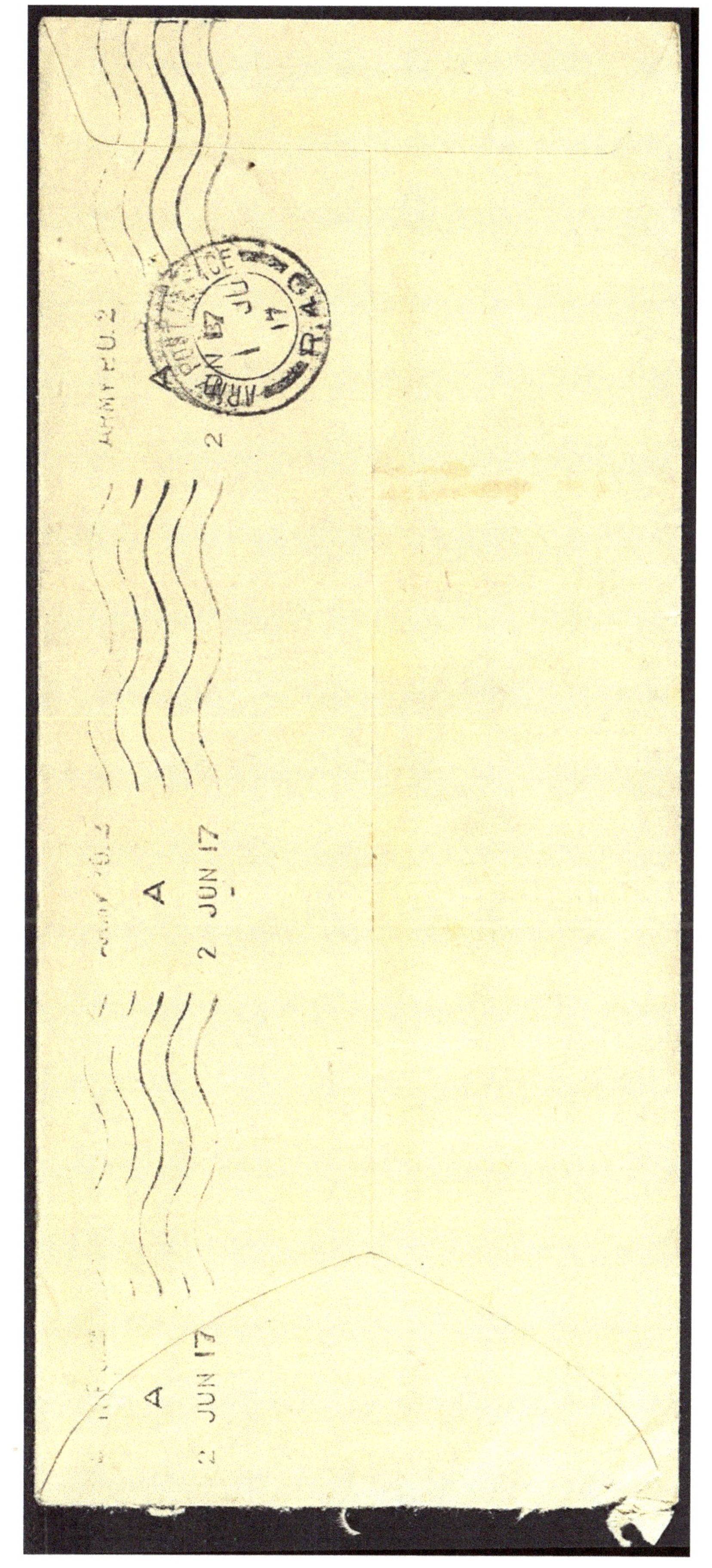

SECRET

Instructions regarding War Diaries and Intelligence Summaries are contained in F. S. Regs., Part II. and the Staff Manual respectively. Title Pages will be prepared in manuscript.

MAY 1917 **WAR DIARY** ~~or INTELLIGENCE SUMMARY~~

(Erase heading not required.)

40TH DIVL SIGNAL COY R.E.

Army Form C. 2118.

Vol / 2

Place	Date	Hour	Summary of Events and Information	Remarks and references to Appendices
MANANCOURT	1		Relief of 121st Bde by 120th Bde in left Sub-sector completed. 119th Bde now have one battalion front on right & 120th Bde one battalion front in centre, 120th Bde two battalion front on left.	
"	2 to 5		Uneventful	
"	6	11 pm	Raid on LA VACQUERIE by 119th & 121st Brigades. Existing communications extended with D Twin to advanced Hdqrs of Artillery & Infantry Brigades. All Battalion lines worked throughout.	
"	7 to 10		Uneventful	
"	11		Uneventful	
"	12		120th Bde relieved by 60th Bde. 120th Bde Hdqrs to SOREL	
"	13		120th Bde relieved Brigade on left in 8th Divn Area.	
"	14		121st Bde relieved Brigade on right in 8th Divn Area.	
"	15 to 22		Uneventful	
"	23		106th Relieved 121st Bde on night. 121st Bde to DESSART WOOD.	
"	24		Uneventful	
	25 to 30		Uneventful	
	31		Commenced 24-wire S-P route towards FINS	

J. Websdale Capt. R.E.
O. Commanding
40th SIGNAL COY. ROYAL ENGINEERS.

2449 Wt. W14957/M90 750,000 1/16 J.B.C. & A. Forms/C.2118/12.

2 SECRET

Instructions regarding War Diaries and Intelligence Summaries are contained in F. S. Regs., Part II. and the Staff Manual respectively. Title Pages will be prepared in manuscript.

WAR DIARY ~~or~~ ~~INTELLIGENCE SUMMARY~~

JUNE 1917

(Erase heading not required.)

40TH DIVL SIGNAL COY R.E.

Army Form C. 2118. 40

Vol 13

Place	Date	Hour	Summary of Events and Information	Remarks and references to Appendices
MANANCOURT	1		120th Bde on GONNELIEU Sub-sector, 121st Bde on LA VACQUERIE Subsector. 119th Bde Reserve in DESSART WOOD.	
"	3		119th Bde relieved 121st Bde on left on night 3rd/4th. Right flank Divn 35th, Left flank divn 59th.	
"	12		121st Bde relieved 120th Bde in GONNELIEU Subsector.	
"	15		Working party of 200 men began digging at night for FIFTEEN RAVINE buried cable route.	
"	19		120th Bde relieved 119th Bde on left.	
"	21		Began laying cable in FIFTEEN RAVINE buried route.	
"	27		~~[illegible]~~ 119th Bde relieved 121st Bde on right	

G. F. Webdale Capt RE
for OC 40th Divl Signal Coy RE.
30-6-1917

2449 Wt. W14957/M90 750,000 1/16 J.B.C. & A. Forms/C.2118/12.

3

D.A.G.

3rd Echelon

Herewith "War Diary" for the month of July 1917

[illegible signature]

Major RE

O.C. 40th Divl Signal Coy RE

40th Divisional Signal Coy.
No.
Date 31-7-17
R.E.

ORIGINAL. 40

Army Form C. 2118.

Instructions regarding War Diaries and Intelligence Summaries are contained in F. S. Regs., Part II. and the Staff Manual respectively. Title Pages will be prepared in manuscript.

WAR DIARY
or
~~INTELLIGENCE SUMMARY~~
(Erase heading not required.)

40th Signal Co. R.E.

JULY 1917.

Vol 14

Place	Date	Hour	Summary of Events and Information	Remarks and references to Appendices
MANANCOURT	2		Commenced 8 pair semi-permanent route from SOREL-LE-GRAND to DESSART WOOD	
"	3		Route completed. Wiring of new Signal Office at SOREL commenced.	
SOREL-LE-GRAND	6		Opened Div'l. Signal Office at 10 am.	
	8		Left (120) Brigade and Centre (119) Brigade moved to vicinity of GOUZEACOURT. Extended their lines with twisted D5 cable.	
	9		Laid D5 pair to Advanced Left Group R.F.A. (1 mile W. of GOUZEAUCOURT). Dismantled part of 8-wire route FINS – DESSART WOOD. Built 2-wire airline from SOREL to QUARRY EXCHANGE (FINS)	
	10		Completed buried route in forward area. 40 pairs 7'-6" deep. 1½ miles.	
	19		Completed new 12 wire semi-permanent route to lateral through Divl. Battle HQ, & picked up 4 Pairs on Corps FINS-GOUZEAUCOURT route as far as Divl Battle HQ.	
	25		Open Advanced Hdqrs South of DESSART WOOD (W 3 c), 12 wire route to QUEENS CROSS, and 8 wire route to REVELON FARM completed.	
	26		Completed 12 Wire lateral from advanced Divl Hdqrs to South.	
	31		Completed 8-wire route from advanced Div HQ. to Heudicourt.	

J. Hebsdale
Capt RE.
for OC. 40th Signal Co. RE.
31-7-1917.

2449 Wt. W14957/M90 750,000 1/16 J.B.C. & A. Forms/C.2118/12.

40

2

ORIGINAL
Army Form C. 2118.

WAR DIARY
or
INTELLIGENCE SUMMARY
(Erase heading not required.)

Instructions regarding War Diaries and Intelligence Summaries are contained in F. S. Regs., Part II. and the Staff Manual respectively. Title Pages will be prepared in manuscript.

40th Signal Co. R.E.

AUGUST 1917.

Vol 15

Place	Date	Hour	Summary of Events and Information	Remarks and references to Appendices
SOREL-LE-GRAND	1		121st Bde on right, 120th Bde on left, 119th in centre. Right flank east of VILLERS GUISLAIN, left flank North of BEAUCAMP.	
SOREL-LE-GRAND	2 to 31		Uneventful.	

H C Summers Capt RE
for O.C. 40th Div. Signal Coy RE
31/8/17

2449 Wt. W14957/M90 750,000 1/16 J.B.C. & A. Forms/C.2118/12.

4

ORIGINAL

Instructions regarding War Diaries and Intelligence Summaries are contained in F. S. Regs., Part II. and the Staff Manual respectively. Title Pages will be prepared in manuscript.

WAR DIARY
or
INTELLIGENCE SUMMARY

(Erase heading not required.)

Army Form C. 2118.

40 D Signal Coy

Vol 16

Place	Date	Hour	Summary of Events and Information	Remarks and references to Appendices
SOREL-LE-GRAND.	1.9.17	–	2nd Lt. G.G. ROUND. RE (attached) proceeded to 3rd Sig Co.	
"	2.9.17	–	Situation normal. Lt C.A. ROBERTSON RE reported from 17th Divl Sig Co for duty as 2nd in Command of 40th Sig Co.	
"	3.9.17	–	Situation normal	
"	4.9.17	–	Situation normal.	
"	5.9.17	–	Situation normal.	
"	6.9.17	–	Situation normal	
"	7.9.17	–	Situation normal. 2/Lt. J.W. MORTON. RE wireless officer 'C' Corps attached for instruction	
"	8.9.17	–	Situation normal.	
"	9.9.17	–	Situation normal.	
"	10.9.17	–	Power buzzer stations established at R.8.c & R.12c. 2.5. (Sheet 57c).	
"	11.9.17	–	Wireless station established at X.3.d. 2.2. (Sheet 57c)	
"	12.9.17	–	Situation normal	
"	13.9.17	–	Signal school moved from BAOURS to MURLU	
"	14.9.17	–	121st Inf Bde H.Qrs moved to W.6.d. 6.5. (Sheet 57c). Communication established by telephone.	
"	15.9.17	–	Situation normal	
"	16.9.17	–	Situation normal.	
"	17.9.17	–	Situation normal.	
"	18.9.17	–	Situation normal.	
"	19.9.17	—	Situation normal	
"	20.9.17	—	16 riding horses of RFA Bde Sections and RA Hqrs detachment replaced by bicycles.	
"	21.9.17	—	2/Lt. J.W. MORTON RE proceeded to rejoin 'C' Corps on completion of instructional course. A/MAJ W.E. KIDNER. MC. RE proceeded to ENGLAND for service in INDIA	
"	22.9.17	—	Situation normal	
"	23.9.17	—	Situation normal	
"	24.9.17	—	Situation normal	
"	25.9.17	—	Situation normal.	
"	26.9.17	—	Situation normal.	
"	27.9.17	—	A/CAPT G.E. CARPENTER MC RE(T) reported from 56th DIVNL SIG Co to command 40th SIG Co vice A/MAJ W.E. KIDNER.	
"	28.9.17	—	2/Lt H.J. THORNTON 3rd Suffolk REGT. proceeded to rejoin his unit	
"	29.9.17	—	Lt. H.J.F. WHITE. 2nd SUFFOLK REGT evacuated sick to 41. Station Hospital	
"	30.9.17	—	Alterations in semi-permanent line system completed	

G.E. Carpenter A/Major MC RE(T)
O/C 40th Divnl Sig Co

2449 Wt. W14957/M90 750,000 1/16 J.B.C. & A. Forms/C.2118/12.

40TH DIVISIONAL SIGNAL COY

Original

Army Form C. 2118.

WAR DIARY
or
~~INTELLIGENCE~~ SUMMARY
(Erase heading not required.)

Instructions regarding War Diaries and Intelligence Summaries are contained in F. S. Regs., Part II. and the Staff Manual respectively. Title Pages will be prepared in manuscript.

Place	Date	Hour	Summary of Events and Information	Remarks and references to Appendices
SOREL LE GRAND	OCT 1	—	Situation normal.	[illegible]
"	" 2	—	Situation normal.	[illegible]
"	" 3	—	Situation normal.	[illegible]
"	" 4	—	Situation normal.	[illegible]
"	" 5	—	Situation normal.	[illegible]
"	" 6	—	Situation normal	[illegible]
"	" 7	—	Situation normal.	[illegible]
"	" 8	—	Situation normal.	[illegible]
"	" 9	—	Div HQ, Sen RA HQ detachment and No 1 Cable Detachment and RFA Sub Sections moved to FOSSEUX. No 2 Sectn (119 Inf Bde) moved to GOUY EN ARTOIS No 3 " (120 Inf Bde) " " BERNEVILLE No 4 " (121 Inf Bde) " " BARLY	[illegible]
FOSSEUX	" 10	—	Company employed on Recreational training.	[illegible]
"	" 11	—	ditto.	[illegible]
"	" 12	—	ditto.	[illegible]
"	" 13	—	ditto.	[illegible]
"	" 14	—	ditto	[illegible]
"	" 15	—	ditto.	[illegible]
"	" 16	—	ditto. Clipping of horses commenced.	[illegible]
"	" 17	—	ditto	[illegible]
"	" 18	—	ditto	[illegible]
"	" 19	—	ditto	[illegible]
"	" 20	—	ditto.	[illegible]

(1)

2449 Wt. W14957/M90 750,000 1/16 J.B.C. & A. Forms/C.2118/12.

40TH DIVNL SIG COY 1

Original

40 D. Signals 40

Vol 17

Instructions regarding War Diaries and Intelligence Summaries are contained in F. S. Regs., Part II. and the Staff Manual respectively. Title Pages will be prepared in manuscript.

(2)

WAR DIARY
or
~~INTELLIGENCE SUMMARY~~

(Erase heading not required.)

Army Form C. 2118.

Place	Date	Hour	Summary of Events and Information	Remarks and references to Appendices
FOSSEUX	OCT. 21	–	Company employed on recreational training.	[initials]
"	" 22	–	ditto.	[initials]
"	" 23	–	ditto	[initials]
"	" 24	–	ditto	[initials]
"	" 25	–	ditto.	[initials]
"	" 26	–	ditto. Clipping of horses completed.	[initials]
"	" 27	–	ditto. LIEUT H.J.F. WHITE SUFFOLK REGT rejoined from hospital and posted to No 4 Cable Detachment at PERONNE.	[initials]
"	" 28	–	RA HQ detachment, No 4 Cable Detachment and RFA Sub Sections withdrawn from line and billeted in PERONNE area.	[initials]
"	" 29	–	DIV. HQ moved to LUCHEUX. No 2 Sectn moved to COUTURELLE No 3 " " " POMMERA No 4 " " " SUS ST LEGER.	[initials]
"	" 30	–	Company employed on recreational training	[initials]
"	" 31	–	" ditto.	[initials]

[signature] Maj. R.E.(T)
O/C 40th Divnl Sig Co.

2449 Wt. W14957/M90 750,000 1/16 J.B.C. & A. Forms/C.2118/12.

Original

Army Form C. 2118.

40TH DIVISIONAL SIGNAL 4 COY

40 D Signals Vol 18

WAR DIARY
or
INTELLIGENCE SUMMARY

(Erase heading not required.)

Instructions regarding War Diaries and Intelligence Summaries are contained in F. S. Regs., Part II. and the Staff Manual respectively. Title Pages will be prepared in manuscript.

Place	Date	Hour	Summary of Events and Information	Remarks and references to Appendices
LUCHEUX	Nov 1 1917	–	Telephone communication established with 119 Inf Bde at COUTURELLE, 120 " " at POMMERA, 121 " " SUS ST LEGER by existing semi-permanent and comic routes.	
			Inf Bde Sectns training in visual.	[initials]
			Hd Sectn training in Cable wagon drill. Recreation in afternoon.	[initials]
"	Nov 2	–	Coy training in visual, cable wagon work and map reading.	[initials]
"	Nov 3	–	Coy training in Cable work. (weather bad for visual). A/CPL FORD. P. 31685 proceeded to ABBEVILLE for Course of instruction in wireless telegraphy.	[initials]
"	Nov 4	–	Coy training in cable work, visual, despatch riding and wireless and power buzzer.	[initials]
"	" 5	–	do do	[initials]
"	" 6	–	do. do.	[initials]
"	" 7	–	do. do	[initials]
"	" 8	–	do. do.	[initials]
"	" 9	–	do. do	[initials]
"	" 10	–	do do	[initials]
"	" 11	–	do do	[initials]
"	" 12	–	do do	[initials]
"	" 13	–	do do	[initials]
"	" 14	–	do do	[initials]
"	" 15	–	do do	[initials]
FOSSEUX →	16	–	Divn Hq moved to FOSSEUX. Communication established with Inf Bdes by D.R. LIEUT. H.J.F WHITE. SUFFOLK REGT. proceeded to join 2nd BDE TANK CORPS for duty.	[initials]

2449 Wt. W14957/M90 750,000 1/16 J.B.C. & A. Forms/C.2118/12.

40TH DIVISIONAL SIGNAL COMPANY

Instructions regarding War Diaries and Intelligence Summaries are contained in F. S. Regs., Part II. and the Staff Manual respectively. Title Pages will be prepared in manuscript.

WAR DIARY
or
~~INTELLIGENCE SUMMARY~~
(Erase heading not required.)

Army Form C. 2118.

Place	Date	Hour	Summary of Events and Information	Remarks and references to Appendices
ACHIET LE PETIT.	Nov 17	–	Divn Hq moved to ACHIET LE PETIT. Inf BDES established at ACHIET LE PETIT area. Communication by telephone. 4 O.R's. proceeded to Third Army Sanitary School St Pol for course of instruction in Sanitary duties and constructional work. (Duration of Course 5 days)	FLC.
"	" 18	–	Company employed on overhauling all technical equipment and refitting	FLC
HAPLINCOURT	" 19	–	Divn Hq moved to HAPLINCOURT area. Telephonic commn established with Inf Bdes at BARASTRE, ROCQUIGNY and BEAULENCOURT.	FLC
"	" 20th	–	Company standing by ready to move at 1 hours notice.	FLC
BEAUMETZ LEZ CAMBRAI	" 21st	–	Div Hq moved to BEAUMETZ LEZ CAMBRAI. Telephonic communication established to 119 Inf Bde at DOIGNIES, 120 BDE LEBUCQIERE, 121 BDE BEAUMETZ LEZ CAMBRAI	FLC
HAVRINCOURT	" 22nd	–	Div Hq moved to HAVRINCOURT opening at 7 pm. Communication to Inf Bdes at GRAINCOURT and LEBUCQIERE by DR only. 40th Div RA Bdes moved to GRAINCOURT area	
"	" 23	–	Telephonic communication established to IV Corps, 119, 121 Inf Bdes, and RFA Groups at GRAINCOURT via existing exchange at HAVRINCOURT Cemetery, and later by direct lines. 120 Bde moved Hqrs to HAVRINCOURT CEMETERY. W/T stns opened at HAVRINCOURT and GRAINCOURT, in communication with Corps Directing Stn at HERMIES. Visual Signal stn established at HAVRINCOURT Cemetery working forward to GRAINCOURT. INF BDE SECTNS established Vis. Commn between GRAINCOURT and BATTN Hqs S of BOURLON WOOD	FLC
"	24	–	Divn in action at BOURLON WOOD. Telephonic Communication broken for 10 hours to Inf Bdes and Arty lines Groups at GRAINCOURT owing to Hostile fire and faulty Cable used in repair of lines. Circuit diagram of lines etc up to midnight 23/24th Nov shown in APPENDIX I. 120 Inf Bde moved to 200 yards N of HAVRINCOURT. Commn by telephone and mounted DR	FLC

2449 Wt. W14957/M90 750,000 1/16 J.B.C. & A. Forms/C.2118/12.

40th Divnl Sig Coy

Instructions regarding War Diaries and Intelligence Summaries are contained in F. S. Regs., Part II. and the Staff Manual respectively. Title Pages will be prepared in manuscript.

WAR DIARY

or

~~INTELLIGENCE~~ SUMMARY

(Erase heading not required.)

Army Form C. 2118.

Place	Date	Hour	Summary of Events and Information	Remarks and references to Appendices
HAVRINCOURT	Nov 25th	—	Divn relieved by 62nd Divn. Circuit diagram of Communications handed over shown in Appendix II.	[initials]
NEUVILLE BOURJONVAL	Nov 26	—	40th Div HQ opened at NEUVILLE BOURJONVAL. Communication established by telephone with 119 Inf BDE at YTRES, 120 Inf BDE at TRESCAULT, 121 Inf BDE at BERTINCOURT. RA. Cable detachment handed over to 62nd Sig Co. (Cpl Brown i/c of detachment).	[initials]
BASSEUX.	Nov 27	—	Div HQ moved to BASSEUX. Telephone Comm established with Inf BDES at BLAIREVILLE, POMMIER and BAILLEULMONT.	[initials]
"	Nov 28	—	Company employed on overhauling Equipment and refitting	[initials]
"	Nov 29	—	do do do.	[initials]
"	Nov 30	—	Company overhauling & refitting. Orders received for unit to be ready to move at 2 hours notice at 5 p.m.	[initials]

[signature] Maj. RE(T)
O/C 40th Divl Sig Co

2449 Wt. W14957/M90 750,000 1/16 J.B.C. & A. Forms/C.2118/12.

40TH DIVNL SIG COY

Instructions regarding War Diaries and Intelligence Summaries are contained in F. S. Regs., Part II. and the Staff Manual respectively. Title Pages will be prepared in manuscript.

WAR DIARY or ~~INTELLIGENCE SUMMARY~~

(Erase heading not required.)

APPENDIX I

Army Form C. 2118.

Place	Date	Hour	Summary of Events and Information	Remarks and references to Appendices

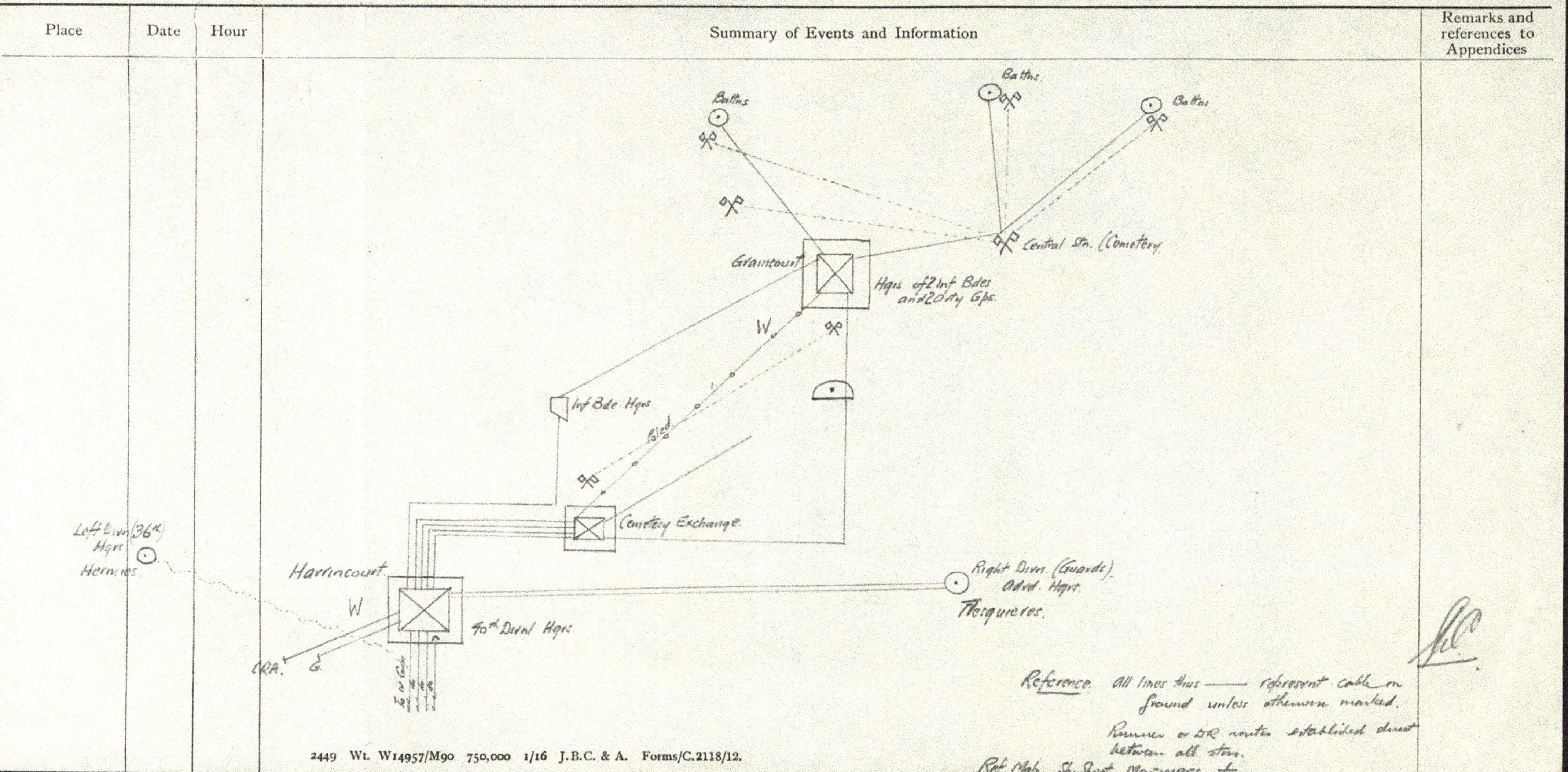

2449 Wt. W14957/M90 750,000 1/16 J.B.C. & A. Forms/C.2118/12.

Instructions regarding War Diaries and Intelligence Summaries are contained in F. S. Regs., Part II. and the Staff Manual respectively. Title Pages will be prepared in manuscript.

WAR DIARY
or
~~INTELLIGENCE SUMMARY~~

(*Erase heading not required.*)

APPENDIX II

Army Form C. 2118.

Place	Date	Hour	Summary of Events and Information	Remarks and references to Appendices

Battns.
Battns.
Battns.
Central Stn (Cemetery)
Graincourt
Hqrs of 2 Inf Bdes and 2 Arty Groups
W
Inf Bde Hqrs.
Poled
Left Divn Hqrs (36th)
Hermies
Cemetery Exchange
Havrincourt
Right Divn (Guards) Advd. Hqrs.
W
40th. Divnl Hqrs
C.R.A.
G.
To IV Corps
29th H.A.G.

Reference. All lines thus —— represent cable on ground unless otherwise marked.
Runner & DR routes established direct between all stns.
Ref Map. Sp Sheet MOEUVRES 1/20.000

2449 Wt. W14957/M90 750,000 1/16 J.B.C. & A. Forms/C.2118/12.

D.A.G.

3rd Echelon

Herewith War Diary for the month of December 1917.

[signature] Capt. O.C. Commanding
40th Signal Coy. Royal [illegible]

Army Form C. 2118.

40 D Signals

Vol 19

WAR DIARY
or
~~INTELLIGENCE~~ SUMMARY

(Erase heading not required.)

40th DIVISIONAL SIGNAL COMPANY.

Instructions regarding War Diaries and Intelligence Summaries are contained in F. S. Regs., Part II. and the Staff Manual respectively. Title Pages will be prepared in manuscript.

Place	Date	Hour	Summary of Events and Information	Remarks and references to Appendices
BASSEUX	Dec 1 1917	–	Company overhauling equipment and refitting.	
"	Dec 2	–	Advance party left for 16 Div Hqrs at BEHAGNIES.	
BEHAGNIES.	" 3	–	Div Hq opened BEHAGNIES at 10 am in relief of 16 Div. in line. System of Communications taken over shown in Appendix I.	
"	" 4	–	Situation normal.	
"	" 5	–	Situation normal. Capt. H.C. SUMMERS granted leave to U.K. for 14 days.	
"	" 6	–	Situation normal. Seven horses and mules received as reinforcements to replace casualties.	
"	" 7	–	Situation normal. Communications being revised. W/T station installed at U 25 b. 5.3 (Sheet 51b SW) working to Corps Directing Stn at Judas Farm. 3 KW. PEL. Set received in exchange for 1 KW. set	
"	" 8	–	Amplifier station installed at U 25 b. 6.3. receiving from Power buzzers at U 14 a 2.8 and U 14 d. 1.5. (Company Headquarters in front line)	
"	" 9	–	Normal work on line maintenance, visual stations etc.	
"	" 10	–	New 8-way route from T 26 a. 5.8 to T 21 d. 5.8 completed, and put through from Div. Hq to Left Bde and Left Group.	
"	" 11	–	Situation normal. Office established at GOMIECOURT, ready for move of Divnl Hqrs.	
"	" 12	–	8 extra lines laid on permanent route from GOMIECOURT to ERVILLERS. for move of Divnl Hqrs	
"	" 13	–	6 extra lines laid GOMIECOURT to BEHAGNIES. for move of Divnl Hqrs.	
"	" 14	–	Divnl Hqrs moved to GOMIECOURT. Bdes and Arty Groups remain in present places. NB. Rt Bde / Rt Group } L'HOMME MORT. Left Bde / Left Gp } St Leger Mill.	

2449 Wt. W14957/M90 750,000 1/16 J.B.C. & A. Forms/C.2118/12.

40th Divnl Sig. Co.

Instructions regarding War Diaries and Intelligence Summaries are contained in F. S. Regs., Part II. and the Staff Manual respectively. Title Pages will be prepared in manuscript.

WAR DIARY
or
~~INTELLIGENCE SUMMARY~~
(Erase heading not required.)

Army Form C. 2118.

Place	Date	Hour	Summary of Events and Information	Remarks and references to Appendices
GOMIECOURT.	Dec 15/17	–	Situation normal.	[initials]
"	" 16	–	do do.	[initials]
"	" 17	–	LIEUT. A.V. FORD granted 14 days leave to UK.	[initials]
"	" 18	–	Normal maintenance work. Buried routes in right bde area overhauled and put into repair.	[initials]
"	" 19	–	Situation normal.	[initials]
"	" 20	–	Following awarded Military Medals in connection with operations at BOURLON WOOD during November. 106648. A/SGT WALKER. 504687 Spr. W.J. VINCENT. 253126 Spr. R.A. GIBBONS. 107165. L/Cpl R. Evans. 106754 A/L/C S. Evans. 107164 L/Cpl J. POWELL. 16045. A/2/Cpl. B. Pick. 172053 L/Cpl. A.G. HINDS.	[initials]
			No 31685 A/Cpl P. FORD. rejoined unit on termination of WIRELESS COURSE at ABBEVILLE	[initials]
"	" 21	–	Situation normal	
"	" 22	–	Normal maintenance work. Visual established between Divn Hqrs. and Stations at Bde Hqrs at ST LEGER MILL and L'HOMME MORT.	[initials]
"	" 23.	–	T/Lt. A.V. FORD. No 17966. Sgt G.E.G. BERRY mentioned in dispatches (Supplement to L.G. 11/12/17)	[initials]
"	" 24	–	CAPT. C.A. ROBERTSON RE. granted 14 days leave to UK.	[initials]
"	" 25	–	Situation normal.	[initials]
"	" 26	–	do do.	[initials]
"	" 27th	–	Bde of 36th Divn ~~[illegible]~~ took over Left Bde Sector 40. Divn. 121 Inf Bde took over Left Bde Sector of 3rd Divn. (Hqrs. L'HOMME MORT.) Communication maintained by telephone and visual.	[initials]
"	" 28	–	Situation normal.	[initials]

2449 Wt. W14957/M90 750,000 1/16 J.B.C. & A. Forms/C.2118/12.

Army Form C. 2118.

WAR DIARY
or
~~INTELLIGENCE SUMMARY~~
(Erase heading not required.)

40th Divisional Signal Coy

Instructions regarding War Diaries and Intelligence Summaries are contained in F. S. Regs., Part II. and the Staff Manual respectively. Title Pages will be prepared in manuscript.

Place	Date	Hour	Summary of Events and Information	Remarks and references to Appendices
GOMIECOURT.	Dec 29th	–	120 Inf Bde. took over Right Bde Sector of 3rd Dvn. Hqrs at MOREUIL. Communication by Telephone via 3rd Divl Hqrs at BEHAGNIES.	[initials]
"	" 30	–	Command of 3rd Divl front taken over by 40th Dvn. & GOC 40 Dvn at 10am. Telephonic Commn established direct to Bdes and Groups as follows. SEE APPENDIX II for diagram of Communications as existing midnight 30.12.17. (120. I/B. Rt Bde. – MOREUIL; (18. AFA Bde) Rt Gp. Centre Bde (121 I/Bde.) / Centre Gp. (42nd REA Bde.) } L'HOMME MORT. Left Bde (119 I/Bde.) L'HOMME MORT Left Gp. (181. REA Bde.) St LEGER.	[initials]
"	" 31.	–	W/T stn established at Rt Bde Hqrs (MOREUIL) – through I Corps D.S. at Judas Farm	[initials] [initials]

[signature] Major RE
O/C 40th Divl Signal Coy

2449 Wt. W14957/M90 750,000 1/16 J.B.C. & A. Forms/C.2118/12.

Army Form C. 2118.

WAR DIARY
or
~~INTELLIGENCE SUMMARY~~
(Erase heading not required.)

40th Divl Signal Coy

Instructions regarding War Diaries and Intelligence Summaries are contained in F. S. Regs., Part II. and the Staff Manual respectively. Title Pages will be prepared in manuscript.

Appendix. I to DEC. 1917

Place	Date	Hour	Summary of Events and Information	Remarks and references to Appendices

Res. Bde.
Locals to
40 DAC.
K.B.S.
Fld. Coy.
Fld Amb.

Res. Bde. Hamelin Court.
To 32nd Divn on Left
To 6 Corps
To 6 Corps
To 3rd Divn on Rt.

FRo. Boyelles.
Locals to
R.E. dump.
Fld. Amb.

W.
Corps. A.S.

Left Bde.
To Bde on Left
To Battns.
To Batteries.
Left Gp.
Vis. Stn.

Pigeon Loft

Behagnies. Exchange
Locals to
I.O.M.
Heavy Arty. Gp.
Labour Coys. etc.

40 Divl. Ex.
40 Divl. R.A. Ex.

Rt Group.
To Batteries.
Rt Bde.
To Battns.
To Bde on Rt.

Left Bn.
Centre Battn.
Rt Battn.
Left Bn.
A.
Rt Battn.
W (Railway Res.
Coy of Rt Bn.

Left Bde.
Locals to
2 Fld. Coys.
Pioneer Battn.
Divl. Observers.
Div. O.P.

Rt Bde.
Locals to
Pigeons.
Bomb. Store.

[Signature illegible]
for 40th Sig Coy

2449 Wt. W14957/M90 750,000 1/16 J.B.C. & A. Forms/C.2118/12.

Army Form C. 2118.

40th Divnl Sig Co

Instructions regarding War Diaries and Intelligence Summaries are contained in F. S. Regs., Part II. and the Staff Manual respectively. Title Pages will be prepared in manuscript.

WAR DIARY
or
~~INTELLIGENCE SUMMARY~~
(Erase heading not required.)

APPENDIX II DEC. 1917

Place	Date	Hour	Summary of Events and Information	Remarks and references to Appendices
Usual Locals on all Exchanges				

FRC.
Left Group.
Left Bde.
Centre Bde
Centre Group
Rt Group
Rt Bde.
W. CRS.
Pigeons.
40 Divn Exch
40 DA Exch
To 3rd Divn on Left
6 Cable 6 Cable
3rd Divn. Hqrs
To 21st Divn on Rt
Advd Exch Inf.
CA Exch.
Battn.
Coy.
A
W

2449 Wt. W14957/M90 750,000 1/16 J.B.C. & A. Forms/C.2118/12.

40th Divnl Signal Co   4

Instructions regarding War Diaries and Intelligence Summaries are contained in F. S. Regs., Part II. and the Staff Manual respectively. Title Pages will be prepared in manuscript.

WAR DIARY
or
~~INTELLIGENCE~~ SUMMARY
(Erase heading not required.)

ORIGINAL. 40 D Signals

Army Form C. 2118. 40

JANUARY 1918

Vol 20

Place	Date	Hour	Summary of Events and Information	Remarks and references to Appendices
GOMIECOURT.	JAN 1/1918.		New line laid to RT BDE (120) at MOREUIL.	
Map Ref. 57 C.	JAN 2/	"	Situation normal. Work proceeding on maintenance of permanent routes, buried ditto etc.	
A.23. D.2.3			LIEUT. A.V. FORD reported from leave.	
"	" 3	"	Nothing of importance	
"	" 4	"		Hes.
"	" 5	"		
BEHAGNIES	" 6	"	Divisional Headquarters opened at Behagnies 12 noon.	Hes.
Map Ref. 57C	"		Enemy attack on Bullecourt Sector, penetrated our trenches, line	
H.2. A.4.5				
"	"	"	re-established during the day. Communications held to Battalion HQ	
"	"	"	during operations, between Battalion and Company HQ, interruptions were	
"	"	"	frequent – due to heavy shell fire.	
"	7	"	Another enemy attack on Bullecourt Sector penetrated our trenches	
"	"	"	on a 200 yards front, line re-established during the afternoon,	Hes.
"	"	"	18 prisoners taken	
"	8	"	Nothing of importance	
"	9			Hes.
	10	"	Situation normal. Maintenance parties at work on open wire & buried routes.	caR.
	11	"	Work in connection with proposed move of Rt. Bde HQ. ~~[illegible]~~ + Rt. Group HQ to C.19 D (Ref: Sheet 57 C N.W) commenced	caR.

2449 Wt. W14957/M90 750,000 1/16 J.B.C. & A. Forms/C.2118/12.

Army Form C. 2118.

WAR DIARY
or
~~INTELLIGENCE SUMMARY~~
(Erase heading not required.)

Instructions regarding War Diaries and Intelligence Summaries are contained in F. S. Regs., Part II. and the Staff Manual respectively. Title Pages will be prepared in manuscript.

Place	Date	Hour	Summary of Events and Information	Remarks and references to Appendices
BEHAGNIES Map Ref. 57C H.2.A.4.5.	12/1/18 13/1/18		Nothing of importance occurred on these dates	C.D.
"	14/1/18		Thaw precautions in force. Divisional/Signal/School opened, number under instruction 9 Officers 139 O.R.	C.D.
"	15/1/18		Thaw precautions still in force.	C.D.
"	16/1/18		Work in camp on defences against enemy aircraft proceeding. Maintenance parties on all permanent telephone routes	C.D.
"	17/1/18		Nothing of importance	C.D.
"	18/1/18		Right Infantry Brigade H.Q. moved to C 19 C from C 9 D (Sheet 57C NW). Additional wireless set erected in left sector.	C.D.
	19/1/18		One additional amplifier and two Power Buzzers erected in Centre Sector	C.D.

2449 Wt. W14957/M90 750,000 1/16 J.B.C. & A. Forms/C.2118/12.

Instructions regarding War Diaries and Intelligence Summaries are contained in F. S. Regs., Part II. and the Staff Manual respectively. Title Pages will be prepared in manuscript.

WAR DIARY
or
~~INTELLIGENCE SUMMARY~~
(Erase heading not required.)

Army Form C. 2118.

Place	Date	Hour	Summary of Events and Information	Remarks and references to Appendices
BEHAGNIES [illegible] H.2.B.4.5.	20/1/18		Heavy maintenance on all open wire routes and buried systems.	C.d.
	21/1/18		Thaw precautions cancelled as from midnight 20/21	C.d.
	22/1/18		Visual communication established throughout the Divisional area	C.d.
	23/1/18		Nothing of importance. ~~[illegible]~~	C.d.
	24/1/18		ditto	C.d.
	25/1/18		ditto	C.d.
	26/1/18		ditto	C.d.
	27/1/18		Bombing raid by enemy aircraft on night 27/28 in neighbourhood of Divnl: H.Q. – No Telephone routes affected.	C.d.
	28/1/18		One small telephone route bombed by enemy aircraft on night 28/29 – no further damage. . .	C.d.
	30/1/18 31/1/18		} Nothing of importance	C.d.

[Signature]
Capt. R.E. for Major R.E. COMMANDING
48TH SIGNAL COY. ROYAL ENGINEERS.

2449 Wt. W14957/M90 750,000 1/16 J.B.C. & A. Forms/C.2118/12.

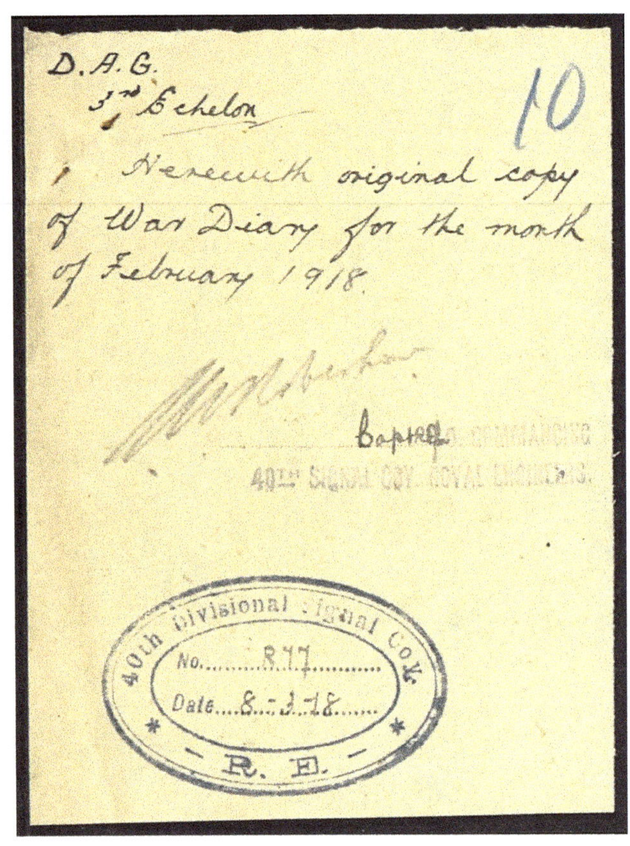

D.A.G.
3rd Echelon

10

Herewith original copy of War Diary for the month of February 1918.

Captain
O. C. COMMANDING
40TH SIGNAL COY. ROYAL ENGINEERS.

Army Form C. 2118.

Instructions regarding War Diaries and Intelligence Summaries are contained in F. S. Regs., Part II. and the Staff Manual respectively. Title Pages will be prepared in manuscript.

WAR DIARY or ~~INTELLIGENCE SUMMARY~~

(Erase heading not required.)

40 ~~Divn~~ Signals Vol 21

Place	Date	Hour	Summary of Events and Information	Remarks and references to Appendices
BÉHAGNIES Ref. 57C. 1/40.000 H2 a 15.55	1/2/18		Hard frost. Maintainance of air line telephone routes heavy.	[illegible]
	2/2/18		Several bays on airline routes broken down. Cable routes laid to overcome difficulty. Thaw commenced. ~~[illegible]~~.	[illegible]
	3/2/18		Lt. G. SHAW 12th West Yorkshire Regt. became attached to this Company on probation.	[illegible]
	4/2/18		Nothing of importance	[illegible]
	5/2/18		Following awarded Military Medal for gallantry in the field. 106816 Cpl. W. MURPHY + 106720 Spr. F. GREEN	[illegible]
	6/2/18 7/2/18 8/2/18 9/2/18		Nothing of importance	[illegible]
	10/2/18		2nd Lt. N.A.J. LAMB RE T/C 3rd Army Signal Coy became attached to this Coy.	[illegible]
	11/2/18 12/2/18		Nothing of importance	[illegible]

2449 Wt. W14957/M90 750,000 1/16 J.B.C. & A. Forms/C.2118/12.

Army Form C. 2118.

WAR DIARY
or
INTELLIGENCE SUMMARY

(Erase heading not required.)

Original

Instructions regarding War Diaries and Intelligence Summaries are contained in F. S. Regs., Part II. and the Staff Manual respectively. Title Pages will be prepared in manuscript.

Place	Date	Hour	Summary of Events and Information	Remarks and references to Appendices
GOMIECOURT Rf/57 C 1/40.000 A 23 d 5.6	13/2/18		Division moved into 6th Corps Reserve. Headquarters ~~[illegible]~~ of Division moved from BEHAGNIES to GOMIECOURT.	cd cd
	14/2/18		Nothing of importance	cd
	15/2/18		Capt. H.C. Summers R.E./T.C. admitted to 6th Corps Rest Station BARLY.	
	16/2/18 17/2/18 18/2/18 19/2/18 20/2/18 21/2/18		Nothing of importance.	cd
	22/2/18		Buried cable scheme at Divnl HQ commenced. Scheme intended to safeguard communications against hostile fire.	cd
	23/2/18 24/2/18 25/2/18 26/2/18 27/2/18		Nothing of importance.	cd

2449 Wt. W14957/M90 750,000 1/16 J.B.C. & A. Forms/C.2118/12.

Army Form C. 2118.

Instructions regarding War Diaries and Intelligence Summaries are contained in F. S. Regs., Part II. and the Staff Manual respectively. Title Pages will be prepared in manuscript.

WAR DIARY

~~or~~

~~INTELLIGENCE SUMMARY~~

(Erase heading not required.)

Original

Place	Date	Hour	Summary of Events and Information	Remarks and references to Appendices
BASSÉUX Ref. 57C 1/40.000 Q 34. d.5.15	28/2/18		Division moved out of 6th Corps Reserve into G.H.Q. Reserve. Headquarters at BASSEUX. Reorganisation of Signal Service under G.H.Q letter O/B 1026 d/ 2.2.18 and 6th Corps No S.Q/393 d/27.2.18 gives following alterations in Divl: Signal Coy R.E. <u>Additions</u>:- 1 Subaltern, 1 Box car + driver A.S.C.M.T; 2 limbered R.E. waggons, 4 draught horses + 2 drivers for the two sub sections attached R.F.A. Brigades <u>Deductions</u>. 1 Riding Horse from each cable section. The following further increase was also authorised for No 5 Section in conjunction with the formation of the ~~[illegible]~~ 40th Battalion Machine Gun Corps. 1 Sgt., 18 Rank & File, 2 draught horses & one limbered G.S. waggon.	[illegible]

[illegible] Capt R.E.
for O. COMMANDING
40TH SIGNAL COY. ROYAL ENGINEERS.

40th Divisional Engineers

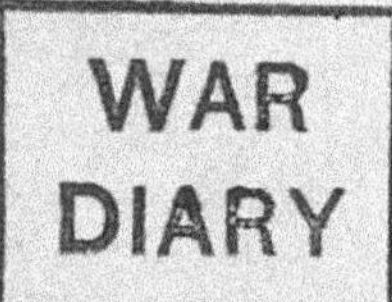

40th DIVISIONAL SIGNAL COMPANY R.E.

MARCH 1 9 1 8

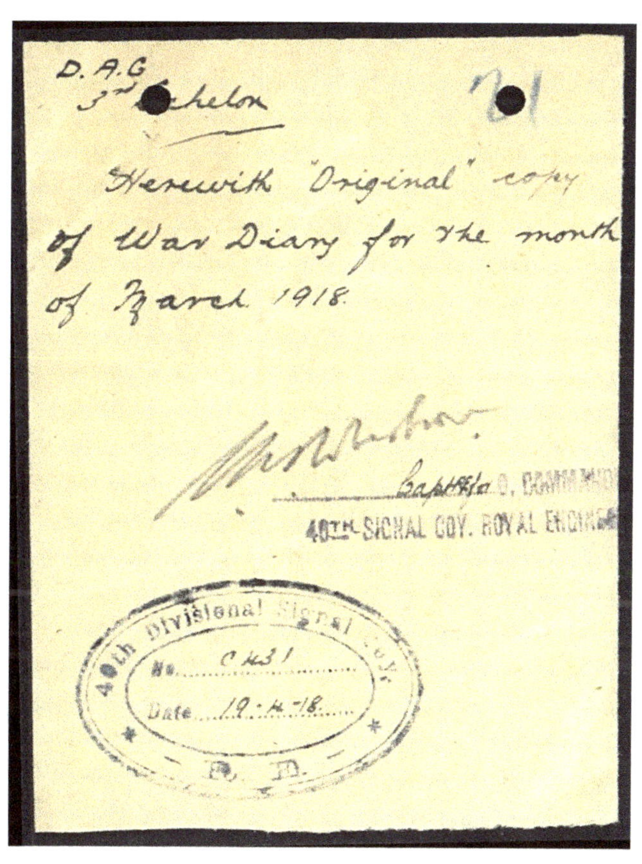
D.A.G
3rd Echelon

21

Herewith "Original" copy of War Diary for the month of March 1918.

Capt. for O. COMMANDING
40TH SIGNAL COY. ROYAL ENGINEERS

40th Divisional Signal Coy.
No. C 431
Date 19.4.18.
R.E.

40th Divisional Signal Coy R.E. ORIGINAL 40 D Signals March 1918 Vol 2 40

Army Form C. 2118.

WAR DIARY
or
INTELLIGENCE SUMMARY

(Erase heading not required.)

Instructions regarding War Diaries and Intelligence Summaries are contained in F. S. Regs., Part II. and the Staff Manual respectively. Title Pages will be prepared in manuscript.

Place	Date	Hour	Summary of Events and Information	Remarks and references to Appendices
BASSEUX 51C Q34 b 5.15.	1/3/18		Lieut. J.C. LLOYD R.F.A. (No. 1 Signal Sub-section R.F.A. Bde) appointed Officer in charge Signal Sub-section 178 Bde. R.F.A.	cal.
"	2/3/18		Lieut F. MEIXNER (Gen: list) transferred from 3rd Army Signal Coy to 40th Divl. Signal Coy R.E. (since admitted to hospital).	cal.
"	3/3/18		Nothing of importance.	cal.
"	4/3/18			
"	5/3/18			
"	6/3/18			
"	7/3/18			
"	8/3/18			
"	9/3/18			
"	10/3/18		2nd Lieut. L. H. MOGRIDGE R.E. 3rd Army Signal Coy attached to this unit as wireless Officer from this date.	cal.
"	11/3/18		Nothing of importance	cal.
"	12/3/18		~~Two~~ Two cable detachments proceeded to forward area. Division in G.H.Q. Reserve.	cal.
"	13/3/18		Nil.	cal.

2449 Wt. W14957/M90 750,000 1/16 J.B.C. & A. Forms/C.2118/12.

40th Divisional Signal Coy R.E.

Instructions regarding War Diaries and Intelligence Summaries are contained in F. S. Regs., Part II. and the Staff Manual respectively. Title Pages will be prepared in manuscript.

WAR DIARY
or
INTELLIGENCE SUMMARY
(Erase heading not required.)

ORIGINAL

Army Form C. 2118

March 1918

Place	Date	Hour	Summary of Events and Information	Remarks and references to Appendices
BASSEUX 51C Q36 a 5.15	14/3/18		Following awarded "1914 Star" C.S.M. M. HEPBURN, Sgt: G.E.G. BERRY, Sgt: R. COULSON, Sgt: H. BLACK 2/cpl. B. PICK, Dvr: C.R. PARISH, Pte ELLSMERE (M.T. ASC attached)	ed.
	15/3/18 16/3/18 17/3/18		Nothing of importance	ed.
	18/3/18		No: 253132 Dvr: E. CRITTON rejoined unit under escort for absence.	ed.
	19/3/18		Nil	ed.
	20/3/18		"	ed.
HAMELINCOURT 51B S29 d central	21/3/18		Divisional H.Q. closed BASSEUX reopened HAMELINCOURT about 5.0 pm. Telephone lines laid to BEHAGNIES and MORY	ed.
	22/3/18		Laddered telephone lines laid to MORY + same diverted to BEHAGNIES. "R.B" Exchange established at ERVILLERS as advanced test point. Divisional H.Q. moved to BUCQUOY 8.15 pm.	ed.
BUCQUOY 57D L10.21.8	23/3/18		"R.B" Exchange closed about 8.0 am. ~~Bdes~~ Infantry Bdes: + Arty: groups moved into GOMECOURT area. Telephone lines laid to GOMECOURT via LONGEAST WOOD and COURCELLES.	ed.

1875 Wt. W593/826 1,000,000 4/15 J.B.C. & A. A.D.S.S./Forms/C. 2118.

40th Divisional Signal Coy R.E.

WAR DIARY
or
INTELLIGENCE SUMMARY
(Erase heading not required.)

ORIGINAL

Army Form C. 2118

Instructions regarding War Diaries and Intelligence Summaries are contained in F. S. Regs., Part II. and the Staff Manual respectively. Title Pages will be prepared in manuscript.

March 1918.

Place	Date	Hour	Summary of Events and Information	Remarks and references to Appendices
BUCQUOY 57D L10 b1.8	24/3/18		Visual communication established between BUCOY and GOMECOURT.	c.d.
	25/3/18		40th Division relieved by 42nd Division.	c.d.
MONCHY-AU-BOIS Lens 11	26/3/18		Divnl: H.Q. established MONCHY-AU-BOIS. Divnl: H.Q. moved to BAILLEULMONT + later to HABARCQ.	c.d.
HABARCQ Lens 11	27/3/18		Divnl: H.Q. established HABARCQ. Divnl. H.Q. moved to WARLUZEL + later to LUCHEUX.	c.d.
LUCHEUX Lens 11	28/3/18		nil.	c.d.
LUCHEUX	29/3/18		Divnl: H.Q. moved to CHELERS	c.d.
CHELERS Lens 11	30/3/18		HIS MAJESTY THE KING visited Divisional H.Q.	c.d.
CHELERS	31/3/18		Divnl: H.Q. moved to MERVILLE. Battle casualties during the month - 1 Officer 5 O.R.	c.d.

M. [signature] Capt R.E.
40th Signal Coy R.E.

1875 Wt. W593/826 1,000,000 4/15 J.B.C. & A. A.D.S.S./Forms/C. 2118.

40th Divisional Engineers

WAR DIARY

40th DIVISIONAL SIGNAL COMPANY R. E.

APRIl 1 9 1 8

Instructions regarding War Diaries and Intelligence Summaries are contained in F. S. Regs., Part II. and the Staff Manual respectively. Title Pages will be prepared in manuscript.

ORIGINAL

Army Form C. 2118 40

40th Divl Signal Coy RE

Vol 23

D.A.G.
3rd Echelon

17th

Herewith 'Original' copy of War Diary for the month of April 1918.

[signature]
Captain R.E. COMMANDING
40TH SIGNAL COY. ROYAL ENGINEERS.

40th Divisional Signal Coy.
No. C.F.18
Date 13-5-18
R. E.

Place	Date	Hour	Summary of Events and Information	Remarks and references to Appendices
1/4/18 CHELERS (SOMME)	1/4/18 (LENS 11)		Divnl: H.Q. moved … MERVILLE. Personnel by bus transport by march …	c.d.
MERVILLE Sheet 36A 1/40000	2/4/18 K29D1.7		Transport arrived a… …ed to move into CROIX du BAC sector. Arm… …patched.	c.d.
CROIX du BAC Sheet 36 1/40000	3/4/18 A6.C 7.5.15		Division moved i… with Divnl: H.Q. at CROIX du BAC and B… …all communication on deep burried system.	c.d.
"	4/4/18		Settled in. Forward wireless stations established	c.d.
"	5/4/18		Nothing of importance.	c.d.
"	6/4/18		O/c Signals attended conference on burried system at STEENWERK	c.d.
"	7/4/18		Nil.	c.d.
"	8/4/18			
"	9/4/18		Heavy enemy bombardment at dawn which continued throughout the morning. Brigades fell back + Divnl: H.Q. moved to DOULIEU at 2.30pm. Later Brigades assembled at LE PETIT MORTIER and at 7.0pm Divisional H.Q. moved to VIEX BERQUIN. Communication by wireless and by cable via DOULIEU	c.d.

1875 Wt. W593/826 1,000,000 4/15 J.B.C. & A. A.D.S.S./Forms/C. 2118.

ORIGINAL

Army Form C. 2118 40

Instructions regarding War Diaries and Intelligence Summaries are contained in F. S. Regs., Part II. and the Staff Manual respectively. Title Pages will be prepared in manuscript.

~~WAR DIARY~~ or INTELLIGENCE SUMMARY

(Erase heading not required.)

40th Divl Signal Coy RE

Vol 23

Place	Date	Hour	Summary of Events and Information	Remarks and references to Appendices
1/4/18 CHELERS (SOMME)	1/4/18 (LENS 11)		Divl: H.Q. moved from CHELERS (SOMME) to MERVILLE. Personnel by bus transport by march route in stages	c.d.
MERVILLE Sheet 36A 1/40000	2/4/18 K29D1.7		Transport arrived at MERVILLE. Division prepared to move into CROIX du BAC sector. Advance party of signallers despatched.	c.d.
CROIX du BAC Sheet 36 1/40000	3/4/18 A6.C 75.15		Division moved into CROIX du BAC sector with Divnl: H.Q. at CROIX du BAC and Bdes: at FLEURBAIX. All communication on deep burried system.	c.d.
"	4/4/18		Settled in. Forward wireless stations established	c.d.
"	5/4/18		Nothing of importance.	c.d.
"	6/4/18		O/c Signals attended conference on burried system at STEENWERK	c.d.
"	7/4/18		Nil.	c.d.
"	8/4/18			
"	9/4/18		Heavy enemy bombardment at dawn which continued throughout the morning. Brigades fell back + Divnl: H.Q. moved to DOULIEU at 2.30pm. Later Brigades assembled at LE PETIT MORTIER and at 7.0pm Divisional H.Q. moved to VIEUX BERQUIN. Communication by wireless and by cable via DOULIEU	c.d.

1375 Wt. W593/826 1,000,000 4/15 J.B.C. & A. A.D.S.S./Forms/C. 2118.

Instructions regarding War Diaries and Intelligence Summaries are contained in F. S. Regs., Part II. and the Staff Manual respectively. Title Pages will be prepared in manuscript.

WAR DIARY

or

~~INTELLIGENCE SUMMARY~~

(Erase heading not required.)

Army Form C. 2118

ORIGINAL

40th Divl. Signal Coy RE

Place	Date	Hour	Summary of Events and Information	Remarks and references to Appendices
VIEUX BERQUIN Sheet 36A. E24. A2.2 1/40,000	10/4/18		Divnl. H.Q. remained at VIEUX BERQUIN with Advanced Divnl. H.Q. at DOULIEU. Telephone communication with Brigades made difficult owing to their H.Q. moving so frequently & at short notice.	C.d.
LA MOT au BOIS 36A. D30. D1.2 1/40,000	11/4/18		Divnl. H.Q. moved back to LA MOT au BOIS at 7.0 pm. and again at 9.0 pm. to AU SOUVERAIN	C.d.
AU SOUVERAIN 36A. D11. B central 1/40,000	12/4/18		Divnl. H.Q. stayed at AU SOUVERAIN. Brigades assembled in neighbourhood of STRAZEELE	C.d.
RENESCURE Sheet 27. T.C 5.90. 1/40,000	13/4/18		Division moved out of the battle with H.Q. at RENESCURE	C.d.
"	14/4/18		Divisional H.Q. moved to LONGUENESSE	C.d.
LONGUENESSE 27 A.S.E. D 15. C central 1/20,000	15/4/18		Nothing of importance.	C.d.

1875 Wt. W593/826 1,000,000 4/15 J.B.C. & A. A.D.S.S./Forms/C. 2118.

Instructions regarding War Diaries and Intelligence Summaries are contained in F. S. Regs., Part II. and the Staff Manual respectively. Title Pages will be prepared in manuscript.

WAR DIARY
or
~~INTELLIGENCE~~ SUMMARY
(Erase heading not required.)

Army Form C. 2118

ORIGINAL

40th Divl Signal Coy RE

Place	Date	Hour	Summary of Events and Information	Remarks and references to Appendices
WIZERNES Sheet 36D NE F2 D8.0 1/20,000	16/4/18		Divisional HQ moved to WIZERNES. Bde HQ remained at TILQUES TATINGHEM and ST MARTIN AU LAERT.	cd
WIZERNES	17/4/18		Refitting in progress. Communication direct and via ST OMER Signal Office.	
"	18/4/18			
"	19/4/18			
"	20/4/18			cd
"	21/4/18			
"	22/4/18			
"	23/4/18			
"	24/4/18			
"	25/4/18			
"	26/4/18			
"	27/4/18			
"	28/4/18			
"	29/4/18			
ST. OMER Sheet 27A SE C12 C5.3 1/20,000	30/4/18		Divl: HQ. moved to ST OMER with Bdes L RYVELD + PROVEN	cd

[signature] Capt R.E.
40th Signal Co R.E.

1875 Wt. W593/826 1,000,000 4/15 J.B.C. & A. A.D.S.S./Forms/C. 2118.

Instructions regarding War Diaries and Intelligence Summaries are contained in F. S. Regs., Part II. and the Staff Manual respectively. Title Pages will be prepared in manuscript.

WAR DIARY or ~~INTELLIGENCE SUMMARY~~

(Erase heading not required.)

ORIGINAL

Army Form C. 2118

4.0

40th Divnl: Signal Coy R.E.

Vol 24

Place	Date	Hour	Summary of Events and Information	Remarks and references to Appendices
ST. OMER	1/5/18		Nothing of importance. Divisional H.Q. ST OMER.	cd
Map Ref. Hazebrouck 5A Scale 1/100,000.	2/5/18			
	3/5/18		Awarded bar to MM Cpl. HEDLEY 7.A. MM	
			Awarded. M.M. Sgt. R. COULSON – L/c A. RAMSEY – Sgt. J.H. FIRTH – 2nd/cpl. R.A. CONSTABLE – Spr J. BIRCHAM – Pnr. A. JONES – Spr. G. GARNETT SGT: H. GODFREY – Spr. A.G. RAMSBOTHAM	cd
			The above awards were made in connection with operations 21-26 Mch 1918	
	4/5/18 5/5/18		Nil	cd
	6/5/18		T/LT. R.K. WOODHOUSE R.E. to ENGLAND on 21 days sick leave.	cd
	7/5/18 8/5/18		Nil	cd
	9/5/18		Seven O.R. joined from Signal Depot as reinforcements.	cd
	10/5/18 11/5/18 12/5/18 13/5/18		Nil.	cd

1875 Wt. W593/826 1,000,000 4/15 J.B.C. & A. A.D.S.S./Forms/C. 2118.

Instructions regarding War Diaries and Intelligence Summaries are contained in F. S. Regs., Part II. and the Staff Manual respectively. Title Pages will be prepared in manuscript.

WAR DIARY

~~or~~

~~INTELLIGENCE~~ SUMMARY

(Erase heading not required.)

Army Form C. 2118

ORIGINAL

20 Divl Signal Coy RE

Place	Date	Hour	Summary of Events and Information	Remarks and references to Appendices
ST. OMER	14/5/18		Reconnaissance of WINNEZEELE LINE carried out with a view to telephone telegraph & all other forms of communication.	cd
	15/5/18		Bde Sections employed in mapping out system of communication for WINNEZEELE line.	
			Awarded bar to MC — T/LT H. CAMPBELL MC. DCM. RE	
			Awarded M.C — a/Capt. C.A. ROBERTSON RE. T/LT R.K. WOODHOUSE RE	cd
			Awarded D.C.M. — Sgt. W. ROOKES M.M.	
			Above awards were made in connection with operations 9–13 Apl: 1918.	
			T/LT H. CAMPBELL MC. DCM. RE to ENGLAND from hospital.	
	16/5/18 17/5/18		Nil.	cd
	18/5/18		Awarded M.M. — Cpl. H.J. EASINGWOOD — Cpl. J. WEBSTER — Cpl. A.H. LAYTON — Cpl R.H. THRELFALL — Spr. E. METCALFE.	cd
	19/5/18		Nil.	cd

1375 Wt. W593/826 1,000,000 4/15 J.B.C. & A. A.D.S.S./Forms/C. 2118.

Army Form C. 2118

WAR DIARY
or
~~INTELLIGENCE SUMMARY~~
(*Erase heading not required.*)

ORIGINAL

40th Signal Coy R.E.

Instructions regarding War Diaries and Intelligence Summaries are contained in F. S. Regs., Part II. and the Staff Manual respectively. Title Pages will be prepared in manuscript.

Place	Date	Hour	Summary of Events and Information	Remarks and references to Appendices
ST OMER	20/5/18		Work in connection with communications for WINNEZEELE	cd
	21/5/18		LINE still in progress. Training scheme drawn up with a	
	22/5/18		view to personnel qualifying for higher ratings.	
	23/5/18		2 O.R. joined from Signal Depôt as reinforcements.	cd
	24/5/18			
	25/5/18			
	26/5/18		Work in connection with WINNEZEELE line + training	cd
	27/5/18		of men in progress.	
	28/5/18			
	29/5/18			
	30/5/18			
	31/5/18			

M. Robertson Capt. R.E.

40th Divl. Signal Coy R.E.

1875 Wt. W593/826 1,000,000 4/15 J.B.C. & A. A.D.S.S./Forms/C. 2118.

40

Army Form C. 2118

Instructions regarding War Diaries and Intelligence Summaries are contained in F. S. Regs., Part II. and the Staff Manual respectively. Title Pages will be prepared in manuscript.

WAR DIARY

~~or~~

~~INTELLIGENCE SUMMARY~~

(Erase heading not required.)

Original

40th Divl. Signal Coy R.E.

Vol 2

Place	Date	Hour	Summary of Events and Information	Remarks and references to Appendices
ST. OMER Sheet 36 D FS General 1/40000	1/6/18		Division under 7th Corps administration. Training of personnel in progress.	[initials]
	2/6/18		ditto	[initials]
	3/6/18		~~ditto~~ Divisional HQ closed ST. OMER & reopened LEDERZEELE	[initials]
LEDERZEELE Sheet 27	4/6/18		Communication to Brigades via Army airline routes	[initials]
S 22 C 3.0 1/40000	5/6/18		Recreational training, horsemastership, drill & technical training.	[initials]
	6/6/18		ditto	[initials]
"	7/6/18		ditto	[initials]
"	8/6/18		ditto	[initials]
"	9/6/18		ditto	[initials]
"	10/6/18		ditto	[initials]
"	11/6/18		ditto	[initials]
"	12/6/18		ditto	[initials]
"	13/6/18		ditto	[initials]
"	14/6/18		ditto	[initials]
"	15/6/18		ditto	[initials]
"	16/6/18		ditto Lt. W. C. HUNT MGCoy. arrived for duty with No. 1 Section.	[initials]

1875 Wt. W593/826 1,000,000 4/15 J.B.C. & A. A.D.S.S./Forms/C. 2118.

Instructions regarding War Diaries and Intelligence Summaries are contained in F. S. Regs., Part II. and the Staff Manual respectively. Title Pages will be prepared in manuscript.

WAR DIARY
or
~~INTELLIGENCE SUMMARY~~
(Erase heading not required.)

Army Form C. 2118

Original

40th Divnl: Signal Coy R.E.

Place	Date	Hour	Summary of Events and Information	Remarks and references to Appendices
LEDERZEELE	17/6/18		Cable detachment sent to RENESCURE for work in connection with possible occupation of WEST HAZEBROUCK line by the Division in the event of an enemy attack on 2nd Army front.	cd
"	18/6/18		Nothing of importance.	cd
"	19/6/18			
"	20/6/18			
"	21/6/18			
"	22/6/18		ditto	cd
RENESCURE Sheet 27 T20 a 9 5 1/40,000	23/6/18		Divnl: HQ closed LEDERZEELE & reopened RENESCURE under 15th Corps administration.	cd
	24/6/18		Communication on airline routes	cd
	25/6/18		Lateral communication between Bdes: via Corps buried system arranged.	cd
"	26/6/18		Box Car of conveyance of W/T stores arrived from 40th Divnl: M.T. Coy.	cd
"	27/6/18		Advanced test point opened & cable run out to Bde. HQ as an alternative means of communication. Corps buried system further utilised.	cd
"	28/6/18			
"	29/6/18		Work on strengthening means of telephone & telegraphic communication in progress.	cd
"	30/6/18			

M. ?Herbert Capt. R.E.
40th Divnl Signal Coy R.E.

1875 Wt. W593/826 1,000,000 4/15 J.B.C. & A. A.D.S.S./Forms/C. 2118.

Instructions regarding War Diaries and Intelligence Summaries are contained in F. S. Regs., Part II. and the Staff Manual respectively. Title Pages will be prepared in manuscript.

WAR DIARY ~~or~~ ~~INTELLIGENCE SUMMARY~~

Original

(Erase heading not required.)

Army Form C. 2118

40

40th Divl. Signal Coy R.E.

Vol 26

Place	Date	Hour	Summary of Events and Information	Remarks and references to Appendices
RENESCURE Map Ref Sheet 27 SW. 1/20000. T21 c.1.6	1/7/18		Work in connection with signal service arrangements for the defence of the West HAZEBROUCK line still in progress.	ECD
"	2/7/18		Nil.	
"	3/7/18		2nd/Lt F.E. RUDDICK. R.E. arrived from 39th Divisional Signal Coy R.E.	ECD
"	4/7/18		Nil	ECD
"	5/7/18		Nothing of importance	ECD
"	6/7/18		"	
"	7/7/18		"	
"	8/7/18		"	
"	9/7/18		"	
"	10/7/18		Recreational training, horsemastership, drill & technical training in progress.	ECD
"	11/7/18		Cable salvage parties at work reeling up circuits not in use.	ECD
"	12/7/18		Nothing of importance.	ECD

Instructions regarding War Diaries and Intelligence Summaries are contained in F. S. Regs., Part II. and the Staff Manual respectively. Title Pages will be prepared in manuscript.

WAR DIARY

or

~~INTELLIGENCE SUMMARY~~

(Erase heading not required.)

Original

Army Form C. 2118

40th Divl: Signal Coy R.E.

Place	Date	Hour	Summary of Events and Information	Remarks and references to Appendices
RENESCURE Map Ref Sheet 27C 1/20000 T21. c 1. 6.	13/7/18		Maintenance of air line + cable communications in progress.	cd
	14/7/18 – 31/7/18		Uneventful	cd

[illegible signature] Capt R.E.

1375 Wt. W593/826 1,000,000 4/15 J.B.C. & A. A.D.S.S./Forms/C. 2118.

Instructions regarding War Diaries and Intelligence Summaries are contained in F. S. Regs., Part II. and the Staff Manual respectively. Title Pages will be prepared in manuscript.

WAR DIARY

~~or~~

~~INTELLIGENCE SUMMARY~~

(Erase heading not required.)

Army Form C. 2118.

ORIGINAL

40th Divisional Signal Coy R.E.

Vol 27

Place	Date	Hour	Summary of Events and Information	Remarks and references to Appendices
RENESCURE Map Ref: Sheet 27 S.W. 1/20000 T21 C1.6	1st Aug. 1918		Maintenance of telephone and telegraph routes laid in connection with the defence of the West HAZEBROUCK line in progress; also training of Signal Service personnel and Battalion Signallers.	
	2nd/8/18		Uneventful	
	3rd/8/18			
	4th/8/18			
	5th/8/18			
	6/8/18			
	7/8/18			
	8/8/18			
	9/8/18			
	10/8/18			
	11/8/18			
	12/8/18			
	13/8/18			
	14/8/18			
	15/8/18			
	16/8/18			
	17/8/18			
	18/8/18			
	19/8/18			
	20/8/18			
	21/8/18			

2449 Wt. W14957/M90 750,000 1/16 J.B.C. & A. Forms/C.2118/12.

Instructions regarding War Diaries and Intelligence Summaries are contained in F. S. Regs., Part II. and the Staff Manual respectively. Title Pages will be prepared in manuscript.

WAR DIARY
or
INTELLIGENCE SUMMARY
(Erase heading not required.)

Army Form C. 2118.

ORIGINAL

40th Divisional Signal Coy R.E.

Place	Date	Hour	Summary of Events and Information	Remarks and references to Appendices
Sheet 27 U.30 C O.7	22nd Aug: 1918		Divisional H.Q. closed RENESCURE (Sheet 27 W 1/20.000 T 21 C 1.6) and reopened U 30 C O.7 Sheet 27 at 5 op.m. This move was made in connection with the relief of the 31st British Division. Communication to Brigades and forward by cable, wireless, pigeons and dogs. Two Brigades in the line one in Reserve.	ed
	23rd/8/18		The success of a minor operation resulted in left Bde: H.Q. moving from SEDEMENT HOUSE (Sheet 36 A NE. D11 D 4.7) to MOLEGHEIN FARM (Sheet 36 A E 10 C) The Right Bde remained at FETTLE FARM (D24 A 7.1 Sheet 36 A) Communication as before.	ed
	24/8/18 25/8/18 26/8/18 27/8/18 28/8/18 29/8/18		Nothing of importance. Maintenance of cable lines very heavy due to the length of lines to be patrolled.	ed
	30/8/18		Machine Gun Battalion and Reserve Bde moved forward to form an advance guard. Communication as before. Enemy withdrawal on this front commenced.	ed
	31/8/18		Line held on one Bde. front. Wireless communication of great assistance during temporary breakdown of telephone & telegraph cables. Possibility of Divisional H.Q. moving up to LA MOTTE (Sheet 36 A NE. D 30 Central) under consideration	ed

[signature] Major R.E.
40th Signal Coy R.E.

2449 Wt. W14957/M90 750,000 1/16 J.B.C. & A. Forms/C.2118/12.

40

Instructions regarding War Diaries and Intelligence Summaries are contained in F. S. Regs., Part II. and the Staff Manual respectively. Title Pages will be prepared in manuscript.

WAR DIARY
or
INTELLIGENCE SUMMARY

(Erase heading not required.)

ORIGINAL

40th Signal Coy RE

September 1918

Army Form C. 2118

9 Sl 28

Place	Date	Hour	Summary of Events and Information	Remarks and references to Appendices
WALLON CAPPEL U30C0.7 Sheet 27	1/9/18		Arrangements for move of Divnl. H.Q. to LA MOTTE (D30C6.4) in progress.	cd
	2/9/18		Divnl. H.Q. closed WALLON CAPPEL + opened LA MOTTE 4.0pm. Field cable telephone lines were extensively used + proved satisfactory. Signal message traffic normal.	cd
LA MOTTE (D30C6.4) Sheet 27	3/9/18		Maintenance of telephone & telegraph routes difficult owing to the large area covered both forward and back.	cd
	4/9/18		State of roads ~~[illegible]~~ in forward area very bad. Despatch rider letter service difficult.	cd
	5/9/18		Forward exchange and despatch rider relay post opened at LE VERRIER (A.19.D) Sheet 36 NW)	cd
	6/9/18		Forward airline circuits begun + existing field cables put up on poles + raised off ground.	cd
	7/9/18 8/9/18 9/9/18 10/9/18		Nothing of importance.	cd
	11/9/18		39th Battn. M.G. Corps arrived in the area.	cd

1875 Wt. W593/826 1,000,000 4/15 J.B.C. & A. A.D.S.S./Forms/C. 2118.

Instructions regarding War Diaries and Intelligence Summaries are contained in F. S. Regs., Part II. and the Staff Manual respectively. Title pages will be prepared in manuscript.

WAR DIARY ORIGINAL

~~INTELLIGENCE SUMMARY~~. 40th Signal Coy R.E.

(Erase heading not required.)

September 1918 (contd:)

Army Form C. 2118.

Place	Date	Hour	Summary of Events and Information	Remarks and references to Appendices
LA MOTTE	12/9/18		Earth faults on telephone cable lines general. Due to bad weather.	[initials]
D30C6.4	13/9/18		Four O.R. arrived from Signal Depot as reinforcements.	[initials]
Sheet 27.	14/9/18		Transport question [struck out]. Lorry + Box Car in workshops for repair	[initials]
			also 2 limber waggons. Abnormal state due to condition of roads.	
	15/9/18		A.B.C. accumulator charging set stationed at advanced post in	[initials]
			LE VERRIER.	
	16/9/18		Wireless communication good but little used.	[initials]
	17/9/18		1 O.R. wounded. Message & D.R.L.S. traffic normal.	[initials]
	18/9/18		Airline routes used for communication well forward – to LE VERRIER (A19D) Sheet 36(NW)	[initials]
			test point. Result, better communication + less earth on lines.	
	19/9/18		Nil	[initials]
	20/9/18		Reconnaissance of routes for building more forward airline or	[initials]
	21/9/18		poled cable routes undertaken	
	22/9/18		Nil	[initials]
	23/9/18		Nil	[initials]
	24/9/18		Nil.	[initials]

(A9175) Wt W2353/P36) 600,000 12/17 D. D. & L. Sch. 52a. Forms/C2118/15.

Instructions regarding War Diaries and Intelligence Summaries are contained in F. S. Regs., Part II, and the Staff Manual respectively. Title pages will be prepared in manuscript.

WAR DIARY ~~or INTELLIGENCE SUMMARY~~. ORIGINAL

(Erase heading not required.)

Army Form C. 2118.

40th Signal Coy R.E.
September 1918.

Place	Date	Hour	Summary of Events and Information	Remarks and references to Appendices
LA MOTTE	25/9/18		Nothing of importance.	cd.
D30 C6.4	26/9/18		ditto	cd.
Sheet 27.	27/9/18		Advanced Divnl: H.Q. opened 9.00am. at A21A6.7 Sheet 36 NW	cd.
	28/9/18		Nothing of importance	cd.
	29/9/18		ditto.	cd.
A21A6.7 Sheet 36 NW.	30/9/18		Divnl: H.Q. opened at A21A6.7 Sheet 36.NW. with rear H.Q. at LA MOTTE.	cd.

[illegible signature] Capt. R.E.

40th Divnl. Signal Coy R.E.

(A9175) Wt W2358/P36 6,0,00 12/17 D. D. & L. Sch. 52a. Forms/C2118/15.

40

ORIGINAL

Army Form C. 2118.

Instructions regarding War Diaries and Intelligence Summaries are contained in F. S. Regs., Part II, and the Staff Manual respectively. Title pages will be prepared in manuscript.

WAR DIARY

or

INTELLIGENCE SUMMARY.

(Erase heading not required.)

40th Signal Coy R.E.
October 1918.

Vol 29

Place	Date	Hour	Summary of Events and Information	Remarks and references to Appendices
A21A6.7	1/10/18		Enemy gradually retiring. Two Brigades in the line one in Reserve.	
Sheet 36 NW.	2/10/18		Forward moves of Brigade H.Q.s followed up by cable wagon.	
	3/10/18		All forward communication by field cable.	
	4/10/18		Advanced test point opened at B8A4.2 Sheet 36 NW.	
	5/10/18		All cable routes forward poled.	
	6/10/18		Nothing of importance.	
	7/10/18		Left Bde came out into support while Right Bde. took over whole line with H.Q at H5D4.1 sheet 36 NW. Advanced test point closed at B8A4.2 + reopened at EPINETTE B27B6.0 Sheet 36 N.W. Forward airline construction begun.	
	8/10/18		1 Officer arrived as reinforcement.	
	9/10/18			
	10/10/18			
	11/10/18		Uneventful.	
	12/10/18			
	13/10/18			

(A9175) Wt W2353/P36 650,000 12/17 D. D. & L. Sch. 52a. Forms/C2118/15

Instructions regarding War Diaries and Intelligence Summaries are contained in F. S. Regs., Part II. and the Staff Manual respectively. Title pages will be prepared in manuscript.

ORIGINAL

WAR DIARY or INTELLIGENCE SUMMARY.

(Erase heading not required.)

40th Divl Signal Coy RE

Army Form C. 2118.

Place	Date	Hour	Summary of Events and Information	Remarks and references to Appendices
A 21 a 6.7	14/10/18		120 Bde closed office at H5d opened at TOUQUET PARMANTIER	
			121 Bde closed office at TOUQUET PARMENTIER and moved to HQ. in line (H11b)	
	15/10/18		Nothing of importance.	
	16/10/18		120 Bde closed office at TOUQUET PARMENTIER opened H11b.	
			121 Bde closed H11b opened I3	
	17/10/18		During operations 121 Bde HQ moved from I3 to I7. Communication becoming difficult both forward and back owing to length of lines. Omnibus circuit D8 cable used.	
	17/10/18		121 Bde closed I7 opened at LA HOULETTE	
			120 Bde closed at H11b opened at HOUPLINES	
			119 Bde closed at A24c opened at TOUQUET PARMENTIER	
			119 closed at TOUQUET PARMENTIER opened at HOUPLINES	
			120 Closed at HOUPLINES opened at J1d	
			121 Closed at LA HOULETTE opened at LA CROIX	
			121 closed at LA CROIX opened at LE MOULIN FERME	
	18/10/18		119 Closed at HOUPLINES opened LA PREVÔTE	
			120 Closed at J1d opened at WAMBRECHIES	

(A9175) Wt W2358/P36 600,000 12/17 D. D. & L. Sch. 52a Forms/C2118/15.

Instructions regarding War Diaries and Intelligence Summaries are contained in F. S. Regs., Part II, and the Staff Manual respectively. Title pages will be prepared in manuscript.

ORIGINAL

WAR DIARY
~~INTELLIGENCE~~ SUMMARY.
(Erase heading not required.)

40 Divl Signal Coy RE

Army Form C. 2118.

Place	Date	Hour	Summary of Events and Information	Remarks and references to Appendices
A21a 6.7	16/10/18		Div HQ. closed A21a6.7 opened at ARMENTIERES	
Armentieres			121 Bde closed LA CROIX opened Lgd	
	19/10/18		120 Bde closed WAMBRECHIES opened ST ANDRE Report Centre opened at WAMBRECHIES	
			Rapid advance. Telephone telegraph Communication difficult owing to distance & State of roads and country	
			Wireless communication to two Brigades. Advanced brigade out of range of apparatus. Mounted Despatch	
			riders used - with relay post at C30 central (Sheet 36).	
	20/10/18		Div H.Q. closed at ARMENTIERES, opened at MOUVEAX with report centre at WAMBRECHIES.	
			Rear Office left at ARMENTIERES.	
MOUVEAUX	21/10/18		Rear H.Q. closed at ARMENTIERES	
	22/10/18		} uneventful.	
	23/10/18		}	
	24/10/18		119 BDE closed at LA PRETOTE opened at BON DIEU	
	25/10/18		121 Bde closed at CROIX opened at LEERS.	
	26/10/18		119 Bde closed at BONDUES opened WATTRELOS. 121 Bde closed at LEERS opened at	
			ESTAIMBOURG (in line)	
LANNOY	27/10/18		Div HQ closed at MOUVAUX at 10am. opened at LANNOY same hour.	

(A9175) Wt W2358/P36) 6,0,000 12/17 D. D. & L. Sch. 52a. Forms/C2118/15.

Instructions regarding War Diaries and Intelligence Summaries are contained in F. S. Regs., Part II, and the Staff Manual respectively. Title pages will be prepared in manuscript.

ORIGINAL

WAR DIARY
~~or~~
~~INTELLIGENCE~~ SUMMARY.

(Erase heading not required.)

40th Divl Signal Coy RE

Army Form C. 2118.

Place	Date	Hour	Summary of Events and Information	Remarks and references to Appendices
LANNOY	27/10/18 (Continued)		Relief of 31st DIV in line completed. Communication by line and Wireless to all Bdes (120 Bde by line via 29th DIV)	[illegible]
	28/10/18		120 Bde closed ST ANDRE opened LANNOY. Adv DIV exchange opened at NECHIN	[illegible]
	29/10/18 30/10/18		Uneventful.	[illegible]
	31/10/18		Remainder of D Arty resting came into line	[illegible]

[signature] II Lieut RE/ for O. COMMANDING 40TH SIGNAL COY. ROYAL ENGINEERS.

(A9175) Wt W2338/P362 600,000 12/17 D. D. & L. Sch. 52a. Forms/C2118/15.

40th Div. Signal Coy RE

Instructions regarding War Diaries and Intelligence Summaries are contained in F. S. Regs., Part II, and the Staff Manual respectively. Title pages will be prepared in manuscript.

11

WAR DIARY ~~or~~ ~~INTELLIGENCE SUMMARY~~.

(Erase heading not required.)

Original

Army Form C. 2118.

Vol 30

Place	Date	Hour	Summary of Events and Information	Remarks and references to Appendices
LANNOY	1/11/18		H.Q. 119 Brigade closed A21a opened at LEERS	
	2 } 3 } 4 } 11/18		Uneventful	
	5/11/18		119 Infantry Bde HQ closed at LEERS opened at H11a99. 121 Infantry Brigade closed H11a99 opened LEERS	
	6/11/18		120 Infantry Bde closed at LANNOY opened at LEERS; 121 Inf. Bde closed at LEERS opened at LANNOY	
	7/11/18		uneventful	
	8/11/18		119 Inf. Bde moved to H11a08	
	9/11/18		Enemy retiring. 120 Inf. Bde moved from LEERS to PECQ. D.W. Report Centre advanced to PECQ	
			119 Infantry Bde moved to CHEMIN VERT	
	10/11/18		120 Infantry Bde advanced to HERINNES	
	11/11/18		Hostilities ceased at 11.00.	
	12/11/18		120 Bde closed HERRINES opened TOUFFLEURS 119 Brigade closed CHEMIN VERT opened HERINNES	
	13/11/18		Uneventful.	
	14/11/18			
	15/11/18		119 Inf. Bde closed HERINNES opened CROIX	

(A9175) Wt W2353/P36 6,0,000 12/17 D. D. & L. Sch. 52a. Forms/C2118/15.

40 Divl Signal Coy RE

Instructions regarding War Diaries and Intelligence Summaries are contained in F. S. Regs., Part II, and the Staff Manual respectively. Title pages will be prepared in manuscript.

WAR DIARY ~~or~~ ~~INTELLIGENCE SUMMARY.~~

(Erase heading not required.)

Original

Army Form C. 2118.

Place	Date	Hour	Summary of Events and Information	Remarks and references to Appendices
LANNOY	16/11/18		Uneventful	
	17/11/18			
	18/11/18			
ROUBAIX	19/11/18		Div Hqrs moved to Rue de Lille Roubaix	
"	20.11.18		"Active Service Army Schools" Courses commenced in Lycee Lulyeck.	
"	21 11 18		Uneventful	
"	22 11.18		do	
"	23 11.18		do	
"	24 11.18		do	
"	25 11.18		do	
"	26 11.18		do	
"	27. 11.18		do	
"	28. 11.18		do	
"	29. 11.18		do	
	30. 11.18		do	

[illegible] Maj
O/C 40th Divl Sig Co

4·0

40th Signal Coy RE. Army Form C. 2118.

Instructions regarding War Diaries and Intelligence Summaries are contained in F. S. Regs., Part II. and the Staff Manual respectively. Title pages will be prepared in manuscript.

WAR DIARY
or
~~INTELLIGENCE SUMMARY.~~
(Erase heading not required.)

Dec: 1918

Place	Date	Hour	Summary of Events and Information	Remarks and references to Appendices
ROUBAIX	1/12/18		Military training - Recreation - Active Service Army Schools in progress.	nil
	2/12/18		ditto	nil
	3/12/18		ditto	nil
	4/12/18		ditto	nil
	5/12/18		ditto	nil
	6/12/18		ditto	nil
	7/12/18		ditto	nil
	8/12/18		ditto	nil
	9/12/18		ditto	nil
	10/12/18		ditto	nil
	11/12/18		ditto	nil
	12/12/18		ditto	nil
	13/12/18		ditto	nil
	14/12/18		ditto	nil
	15/12/18		ditto	nil
	16/12/18		ditto	nil

Instructions regarding War Diaries and Intelligence Summaries are contained in F. S. Regs., Part II, and the Staff Manual respectively. Title pages will be prepared in manuscript.

WAR DIARY
or
~~INTELLIGENCE SUMMARY.~~
(Erase heading not required.)

Army Form C. 2118.

40th Signal Coy R.E.

Dec: 1918

Place	Date	Hour	Summary of Events and Information	Remarks and references to Appendices
ROUBAIX	17/12/18		Military training - Recreation and Active Service Army Schools in progress.	cd
	18/12/18		ditto	cd
	19/12/18		ditto	cd
	20/12/18		ditto	cd
	21/12/18		ditto	cd
	22/12/18		~~G.O.C. inspected the Coy on parade~~ ditto	cd
	23/12/18		G.O.C. 40th Division inspected the Coy on parade	cd
	24/12/18		Treated as holidays. Signal offices open at certain specified periods	cd
	25/12/18		during the days	cd
	26/12/18			cd
	27/12/18		Military training - Recreation an Active Service Army Schools in progress.	cd
	28/12/18		ditto	cd
	29/12/18		ditto	cd
	30/12/18		ditto	cd
	31/12/18		ditto	cd

[signature] Capt R.E.

40th SIGNAL COY. ROYAL ENGINEERS

(A9175) Wt W2353/P36 620,000 12/17 D. D. & L. Sch. 52a. Forms/C2118/15.

40

Instructions regarding War Diaries and Intelligence Summaries are contained in F. S. Regs., Part II, and the Staff Manual respectively. Title pages will be prepared in manuscript.

WAR DIARY
or
INTELLIGENCE SUMMARY.
(Erase heading not required.)

Army Form C. 2118.

40 D Signal

8/8 32

Place	Date	Hour	Summary of Events and Information	Remarks and references to Appendices
ROUBAIX	Jany 1 6 28		Education under Army Schools Arrangements – Recreation Training	
			Demobilization proceeding normally – average 3 men weekly sent from unit.	
	2-31.		Demobilization of Signal Service personnel proceeding under Signal officer in chief	
			[signature] Captain for C 40 Div Sig Co R.E.	

(A9175) Wt W2353/P36 600,000 12/17 D. D. & L. Sch. 52a. Forms/C2118/15.

Army Form C. 2118.

40

WAR DIARY
or
~~INTELLIGENCE SUMMARY.~~ 40th Signal Coy, R.E.
February 1919

(Erase heading not required.)

Instructions regarding War Diaries and Intelligence Summaries are contained in F. S. Regs., Part II. and the Staff Manual respectively. Title pages will be prepared in manuscript.

3

Place	Date	Hour	Summary of Events and Information	Remarks and references to Appendices
ROUBAIX Sheet 37 NW	1/2/19		Divl. H.Q. at ROUBAIX - Divl. Artillery H.Q. WAMBRECHIES Infantry Bde. H.Q. [illegible] CROIX and LANNOY. (Ref: Sheets 36NE + 37NW) Communication as usual. Demobilisation of personnel & horses in progress.	[illegible]
"	2/2/19		Nothing of importance	[illegible]
"	3/2/19		ditto	[illegible]
"	4/2/19		ditto	[illegible]
"	5/2/19		ditto	[illegible]
"	6/2/19		ditto	[illegible]
"	7/2/19		2/Lt. MOODY proceeded to U.K. on leave	[illegible]
"	8/2/19		Nothing of importance	[illegible]
"	9/2/19		ditto	[illegible]
"	10/2/19		ditto	[illegible]
"	11/2/19		ditto	[illegible]
"	12/2/19		Lt. Aylott & Lt. Grimes to U.K. for demobilisation	[illegible]
"	13/2/19		Maj. G. L. Carpenter M.C. R.E.T. to U.K. for demobilisation	[illegible]

Army Form C. 2118.

Instructions regarding War Diaries and Intelligence Summaries are contained in F. S. Regs., Part II, and the Staff Manual respectively. Title pages will be prepared in manuscript.

WAR DIARY
or
~~INTELLIGENCE SUMMARY.~~
(Erase heading not required.)

40th Signal Coy R.E.
February 1919.

Place	Date	Hour	Summary of Events and Information	Remarks and references to Appendices
ROUBAIX	14/2/19		Nothing of importance	[illegible]
Sheet 37 NW	15/2/19		ditto	[illegible]
"	16/2/19		ditto	[illegible]
"	17/2/19		ditto	[illegible]
"	18/2/19		Infantry Bde Signal Sections concentrated with H.Q. + No. 1 Signal Sections to facilitate demobilisation. R.F.A Bde Subsections also concentrated with H.Q. Section Divl Artillery. Communication uninterrupted.	[illegible]
"	19/2/19		Nothing of importance	[illegible]
"	20/2/19		ditto	[illegible]
"	21/2/19		ditto	[illegible]
"	22/2/19		ditto	[illegible]
"	23/2/19		ditto	[illegible]
"	24/2/19		ditto	[illegible]
"	25/2/19		ditto	[illegible]
"	26/2/19		ditto	[illegible]

(A9175) Wt W2358/P361 600,000 12/17 D. D. & L. Sch. 52a. Forms/C2118/15.

Army Form C. 2118.

Instructions regarding War Diaries and Intelligence Summaries are contained in F. S. Regs., Part II. and the Staff Manual respectively. Title pages will be prepared in manuscript.

WAR DIARY
or
~~INTELLIGENCE SUMMARY.~~
(Erase heading not required.)

40th Signal Coy R.E.
February 1919.

Place	Date	Hour	Summary of Events and Information	Remarks and references to Appendices
ROUBAIX (Sheet 37 NW)				
"	27/2/19		Nothing of importance.	[illegible]
"	28/2/19		Lt. Ford M.C. R.E. and Lt. Hunt R.E. to U.K. for demobilisation.	[illegible]

[illegible signature]
Capt. R.E.

40th Signal Coy. Royal Engineers

(A9175) Wt W2358/P36 600,000 12/17 D. D. & L. Sch. 52a. Forms/C2118/15

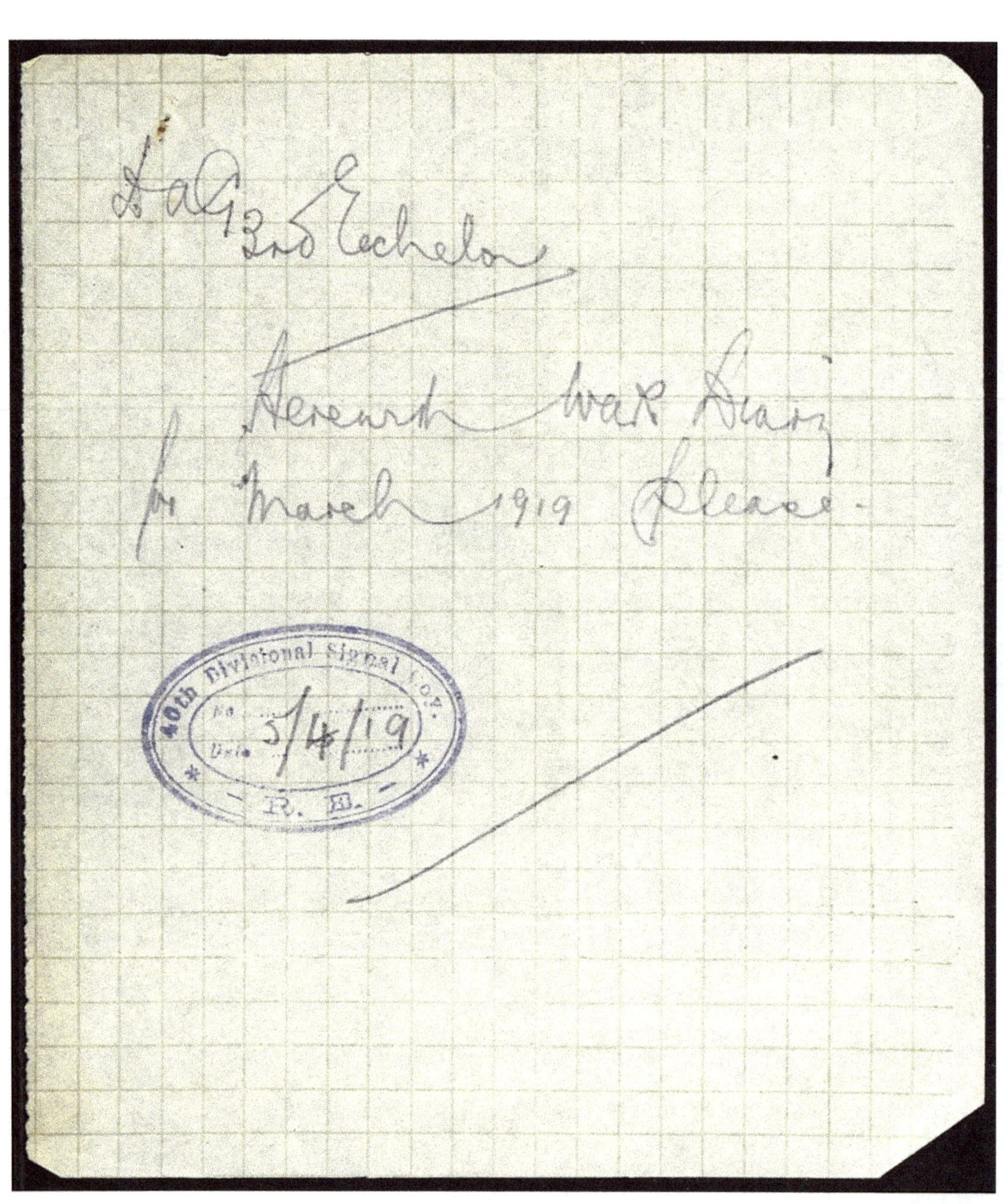
D.A.G. 3rd Echelon

Herewith War Diary for March 1919 please.

40th Divisional Signal Coy.
No. ......
Date 5/4/19
– R. E. –

Army Form C. 2118.

40

Instructions regarding War Diaries and Intelligence Summaries are contained in F. S. Regs., Part II, and the Staff Manual respectively. Title pages will be prepared in manuscript.

WAR DIARY
or
~~INTELLIGENCE SUMMARY.~~
(Erase heading not required.)

40th Signal Coy R.E.
Mch: 1919.
Vol 34

Place	Date	Hour	Summary of Events and Information	Remarks and references to Appendices
ROUBAIX 36/25 B20.70	1/3/19		Demobilisation of both men and animals in progress	cd
	2/3/19		ditto	cd
"	3/3/19		Capt A/MAJ: C.F. CHUTE M.C. R.E. (S.R.) assumed command of the Company	cd
"	4/3/19		Information received to demobilise down to cadre "A"	cd
"	5/3/19		Signal communications within the division confined to D.R.L.S. and	
"			on telephone for Artillery and Infantry Bde. H.Q.	cd
"	6/3/19		Personnel employed on Salvage work on a large scale	
"			(5th Army Sub area 4) withdrawn owing to demobilisation. Small	
"			salvage parties still at work in neighbourhood of ROUBAIX 36/25 B20.70.	cd
"	7/3/19		Recreational training and amusements for personnel on	
"			Mondays Wednesdays and Saturdays	cd
"	8/3/19		Nothing of importance.	cd
	9/3/19		ditto	cd
	10/3/19		ditto	cd
	11/3/19		ditto	cd
	12/3/19		ditto	cd

(A9175) Wt W2358/P36 600,000 12/17 D. D. & L. Sch. 52a. Forms/C2118/15.

Instructions regarding War Diaries and Intelligence Summaries are contained in F. S. Regs., Part II. and the Staff Manual respectively. Title pages will be prepared in manuscript.

WAR DIARY
or
~~INTELLIGENCE SUMMARY.~~
(Erase heading not required.)

Army Form C. 2118.

40th Signal Coy R.E.
Mch: 1919

Place	Date	Hour	Summary of Events and Information	Remarks and references to Appendices
ROUBAIX 36/L5B20.70	13/3/19		Nothing of importance.	[initials]
	14/3/19		ditto	[initials]
	15/3/19		ditto	[initials]
	16/3/19		ditto	[initials]
	17/3/19		ditto	[initials]
	18/3/19		ditto	[initials]
	19/3/19		ditto	[initials]
	20/3/19		ditto	[initials]
	21/3/19		ditto	[initials]
	22/3/19		ditto	[initials]
	23/3/19		The last batch of horses and mules despatched to Animal Collecting Camps, thus reducing the Coy to Cadre A so far as horse transport is concerned	[initials]
	24/3/19		Nothing of importance	[initials]
	25/3/19		Divnl: HQ closed ROUBAIX 36/L5B20.70 & opened CROIX 36/L10A90.70 but Coy. HQ remained at ROUBAIX. 36/L5B20.70	[initials]
	26/3/19		Nothing of importance.	[initials]
	27/3/19		ditto.	[initials]

Instructions regarding War Diaries and Intelligence Summaries are contained in F. S. Regs., Part II. and the Staff Manual respectively. Title pages will be prepared in manuscript.

WAR DIARY
or
~~INTELLIGENCE SUMMARY.~~
(Erase heading not required.)

Army Form C. 2118.

40th Signal Coy R.E.
Mch. 1919.

Place	Date	Hour	Summary of Events and Information	Remarks and references to Appendices
ROUBAIX	28/3/19		Nothing of importance	[illegible]
"	29/3/19		ditto	[illegible]
"	30/3/19		ditto	[illegible]
"	31/3/19		ditto	[illegible]

[illegible signature] Capt. R.E.
40th Signal Coy R.E.

(A9175) Wt W2358/P36 600,000 12/17 D. D. & L. Sch. 52a. Forms/C2118/15.

www.ingramcontent.com/pod-product-compliance
Lightning Source LLC
Chambersburg PA
CBHW081553160426
43191CB00011B/1915

* 9 7 8 1 4 7 4 5 1 9 4 3 4 *